SOCIOLOGY FOR PHARM

Sociology for Pharmacists

An Introduction

Geoffrey Harding

Sarah Nettleton

Kevin Taylor

MACMILLAN

First published 1990 by
THE MACMILLAN PRESS LTD
Houndmills, Basingstoke, Hampshire RG21 2XS
and London
Companies and representatives
throughout the world

ISBN 0-333-49764-3 hardcover
ISBN 0-333-49765-1 paperback

A catalogue record for this book is available
from the British Library.

Printed in Hong Kong

11	10	9	8	7	6	5	4	3
03	02	01	00	99	98	97	96	95

To Sally Ann and Pauline

Contents

List of Tables

Acknowledgement

We are grateful to Boots The Chemists for their assistance towards the production of this book. We would also like to thank Ann Oakley for her comments on an earlier draft of the book.

Preface

This book is intended to acquaint the reader with some of the basic theories and concepts of medical sociology and their application to aspects of pharmaceutical service delivery. We have written this book in response to the recognition that social science can contribute towards equipping pharmacists for practice in the 1990s and beyond. We have adopted an inter-disciplinary approach to the preparation of this book. The topics covered are by no means exhaustive. Rather we have addressed those issues which we consider collectively, as pharmacist, sociologists, and as health care consumers, to be most important.

In chapter one we introduce the subject of sociology and discuss the developments within pharmacy which have led to calls for subjects such as sociology to be included in the pharmacy undergraduate degree curriculum. In chapter two we examine pharmacists' roles and activities in the light of the Nuffield Report on Pharmacy. We also examine the implications of that report and of government proposals on health policy, for the future practice of pharmacy. Sociological perspectives on the experience of illness, and illness behaviour are explored in chapters three and four, and we note that the presence of symptom(s) alone may not result in an individual seeking help or treatment from a health professional. Chapters five and six consider the ways in which health status, and the experience of illness are influenced by such factors as social class, gender and ethnicity. The potentially contentious issue of whether pharmacy, when examined from a sociological perspective, can or can not be considered a full profession is covered in chapter seven. In chapters eight and nine we consider the issues of health education and the pharmacist's role in health promotion. Chapter ten is devoted to a brief introduction to some methodological issues in social research, and incorporates some guidance as to how these issues may be applied to research in the social aspects of pharmacy.

As such we hope this book will be used by students, academic pharmacists and practising pharmacists alike. Moreover, we hope it will stimulate the development of sociologically informed research in social aspects of the practice of pharmacy.

1 Social Science and Pharmacy

In recent years the role of the pharmacist has undergone significant changes. As the number of available proprietary medicines has increased, the day-to-day activities of pharmacists have as a consequence altered so that for he, and increasingly she, the actual process of compounding and formulating medicines has become less demanding on their time than in the past. A corollary of this development has been the opportunity for pharmacists to promote themselves as primary health care professionals, from whom medical advice may be sought, prior to, in addition to, or instead of visiting a medical practitioner.

The time when pharmacists could spend their days closeted in the dispensary at the back of a shop are long gone. With the increasing tendency of the pharmaceutical manufacturing industry to present medicinal products in packages suitable for dispensing direct to the consumer, even those pharmacists with the heaviest dispensing loads are finding that they have more and more time available for taking on what has been referred to as the pharmacist's 'extended role'. This 'extended role' requires the pharmacist to interact directly with the public, offering a range of services including health care advice, information, recommendations, directions and instruction, in addition to ensuring that people receive the correct medication and understand how to use their medicines correctly.

The undergraduate curriculum taught in British schools of pharmacy has traditionally focused on the basic and applied sciences including pharmaceutical chemistry, pharmaceutics, pharmacognosy, and pharmacology (Harding, 1988). In the 1970s and 1980s the curriculum in most schools was expanded to introduce the subject area of 'clinical pharmacy'. Clinical pharmacy draws on the knowledge of drugs and disease as taught within a framework of the basic sciences and then relates this knowledge directly to the clinical requirements of patients.

The realisation within the pharmaceutical profession that its

1

members were being increasingly called upon to give medical advice, 'counsel' patients and disseminate health education messages has resulted in a new concept, that of 'Pharmacy practice'. Pharmacy practice is an all-embracing term which describes a wide range of activities involved in the provision of pharmaceutical service delivery. Consequently it incorporates 'clinical pharmacy' and also involves an appreciation of pharmacy in the wider context of health care delivery.

In recognition that pharmacists are increasingly assuming the role of primary health care professionals, and are not just dispensers of medicines and suppliers of appliances, students of pharmacy are now being encouraged to acquire new skills as communicators, educators and advisors. 'Behavioural Science' has been identified as having a significant contribution to make in this training of future pharmacists. The Nuffield Inquiry in 1986 (Nuffield Committee of Inquiry into Pharmacy), which closely examined all areas of pharmacy, indicated that 'behavioural science' should be incorporated into the pharmacy undergraduate curriculum. The term 'behavioural science' denotes the scientific study of human behaviour and although it is most frequently associated with the discipline of psychology, implicitly it includes other disciplines concerned with the study of people and society, such as sociology and anthropology. In this book we are concerned specifically with the application of sociology to the practice of pharmacy. Sociology explains an individual's actions as a social phenomenon. That is to say, behaviour is explained and governed by the society in which we live. For this reason sociologists prefer to use the term 'social action' rather than 'behaviour'. Other areas included under the umbrella term 'behavioural science', for example social psychology and interpersonal communication, have been covered adequately elsewhere (Hargie *et al.*, 1987; Dickson *et al.*, 1989) and are beyond the remit of this book.

The medical profession has recognised the value of looking at health and illness from a sociological perspective. Indeed sociology as applied to medicine is taught routinely in medical and dental schools in the United Kingdom (Behavioural Sciences Group 1987). The introduction of medical sociology into the pre-clinical medical courses was a significant departure from those subjects previously taught in such courses. The traditional teaching had tended to be based almost exclusively on detailed anatomical, histological and physiological studies of tissues and organs of the body. It could similarly be argued that the teaching of pharmacy has traditionally concentrated on the 'drug entity', its derivation from plant and animal sources, its action on the body, its disposition within the body, its chemical nature and formulation into dosage forms.

Thus as educational institutions respond to the Nuffield Inquiry and the developing role of the pharmacist in the provision of health care, it has been suggested that aspects of sociology should be incorporated into the pharmacy undergraduate curriculum in order to adequately prepare pharmacy students for their future role. A working party of the Royal Pharmaceutical Society's Education Committee has investigated this suggestion. The report of this working party (Working Party on Social and Behavioural Science 1989) makes thirteen recommendations with respect to the pharmacy degree course, the main recommendation being that, 'all schools of pharmacy should include teaching in the social science aspects of pharmacy, in the undergraduate pharmacy degree course'.

1.1 WHAT IS SOCIOLOGY?

The boundaries of the discipline of sociology are difficult to define, in part because of the diverse and diffuse nature of its subject matter, i.e. people and society, and also because within the discipline of sociology itself there are many different approaches or perspectives; indeed there are many different types of sociology. However it is probably true to say that all sociologists share some basic assumptions. One such assumption is that human behaviour is conditioned by our social environment. How people act, think, and behave is a result of the way in which they have been 'brought up'. Social rules and social norms have become internalised, that is they become internal to the individual and are thus self-imposed rather than imposed by others. Norms refer to actions that are expected or considered 'normal' in any given society. For example, if we were to visit our general practitioner we might expect him or her to sit by his or her desk, ask us the reason for our visit, what our problem is, and we would expect to respond. If the general practitioner was to start playing a flute, he or she would be breaking social norms or expectations.

Another basic assumption in sociology is that in order to understand society it is insufficient to take an individualistic point of view. That is, it is not sufficient to understand or explain people's actions solely through the behaviour of the individual or individuals concerned. It is necessary to take a wider social perspective and understand the social forces that impinge on, influence, or interact with the individual. These social forces are usually beyond the control of the individual. To develop an appreciation of the interaction of the individual in society is to come close to what the sociologist, Wright-Mills (1959) calls the sociological imagination, that is, 'the urge to know the social and historical meaning of the individual in society'. For example, if only a few hundred people in our country were unemployed we might consider the reason for their being out of work as having something to do with their own circumstances, or as a reflection on them as individuals. If over three million people, however, are out of work, we recognise that there is something else going on in society independently of those individuals who are unemployed. We can consider society on two levels: the individual level, and the collective or structural level. The sociologist aims to understand the interaction between these two. Let us take another example from Wright-Mills:

> Consider marriage. Inside a marriage a man and a woman may experience personal troubles, but when the divorce rate during the first four years of marriage, is two hundred and fifty out of every thousand attempts, this is an indication of a structural issue, having to do with the institution of marriage and family, and other institutions that bear upon them.

We can see, then, that individuals and relationships between individuals are influenced by structural, i.e. broader social, economic and political circumstances.

Sociology is not just about the collection of facts and information; it is concerned more with understanding and interpretation. It can be confusing and daunting for those who are not used to this way of learning and thinking. What the sociologist looks at is often familiar, concerning our everyday activities. 'The sociologist does not look at phenomenon that no one else is aware of, but he or she looks at the phenomenon in a different way' (Berger, 1966).

1.2 SOCIOLOGY AS APPLIED TO PHARMACY

Medical sociologists study health and illness as social phenomena, and have examined the activities of health professionals such as doctors, dentists, nurses, health visitors and midwives. Until recently, however, pharmacists have been virtually neglected by sociologists.

Pharmacy is in the process of rapid change and development, with pharmacists being encouraged to take on new roles including that of community-based health promoters. Assuming these new roles presents a number of difficulties for pharmacists; for instance not all individuals will respond to symptoms in the same way, not everyone has faith in orthodox medicine, and the need to seek treatment is not necessarily a top priority for everyone and may compete with other factors such as work and family commitments, or difficulties of transport and mobility.

An appreciation of these considerations allied with the pharmacist's traditional knowledge of drugs and drug therapy will serve to assist in providing advice or treatment appropriate to meet the needs of a particular patient. Medical sociology can give an insight into the individual's responses to illness through an appreciation of how a patient's own feelings about their health and illness arise, and the motivations and constraints that have an influence on their using or not using of medicines and the health care services.

Further Reading

Bilton, T. *et al.* (1987) *Introductory Sociology*, London, Macmillan.
Giddens, A. (1989) *Sociology*, Cambridge, Polity Press.

References

Behavioural Sciences Group (1987) *Compendium of Behavioural Science Teaching at Medical and Dental Schools in the United Kingdom*, University of Glasgow.
Berger, P. (1966) *Invitation to Sociology: A Humanistic Perspective*, Harmondsworth, Penguin.
Dickson, D. A., Hargie, O. and Morrow, N. C. (1989) *Communication Skills Training for Health Professionals*, London, Chapman and Hall.
Harding, G. (1988) Behavioural Science and Pharmacy, *Pharmaceutical Journal*, 242: 124.

Hargie, O., Sanders, C. and Dickson, D. A. (1987) *Interpersonal Communication Skills*, London, Croom Helm.

Nuffield Committee of Inquiry into Pharmacy (1986) *Pharmacy: a report to the Nuffield Foundation*, London, Nuffield Foundation.

Working Party on Social and Behavioural Science (1989) London, The Royal Pharmaceutical Society.

Wright-Mills, C. (1959) *The Sociological Imagination*, New York, Oxford University Press.

2 The Development of Pharmacy: Setting the Scene

In this chapter we will attempt to illustrate that the role of the pharmacist has been evolving in recent years and that pharmacists are now expected by both the public and the government to provide a wider range of services than in the past. We have not attempted to provide here a detailed historical account of the development of pharmacy from its earliest history through to the present day (a brief outline of the history of pharmacy can be found in Chapter 7), nor do we provide an exhaustive account of pharmacists' day-to-day activities. Such information is already available elsewhere (Stone and Curtis, 1989).

In 1983 a major review of the pharmaceutical profession was undertaken. The Committee of Inquiry into Pharmacy, commonly referred to as the 'Nuffield Inquiry', was an independent investigation into the practice of pharmacy in Great Britain. The Inquiry received submissions from a wide range of sources including pharmacists from all branches of the profession, and representatives of the British Medical Association, the Consumers' Association, and Societies representing a broad spectrum of other health care professionals. The terms of reference for the inquiry were 'To consider the present and future structure of the practice of pharmacy in its several branches and its potential contribution to health care and to review the education and training of pharmacists accordingly.' The report of the inquiry was published in March 1986 (Nuffield Committee of Inquiry, 1986). Ninety-six conclusions and recommendations were contained in the report, relating to community, hospital and industrial pharmacy, undergraduate, postgraduate and continuing education, pharmacy practice research and the Pharmaceutical Society. Pharmacy as a profession is in the process of responding to and implementing these recommendations.

Currently there are over thirty thousand registered pharmacists in Great Britain, the majority working in community or hospital pharmacy: of those in paid employment, 73 per cent practise in the community and 16 per cent practise in hospital pharmacies (Table 2.1).

In the past few decades there has been an increase in the proportion of women practising pharmacy. Manpower studies have indicated that approximately 60 per cent of entrants into schools of pharmacy are now women (Elworthy, 1986). These studies have also indicated that after having children, an increased proportion of women work in community pharmacy.

2.1 HOSPITAL PHARMACY

Until the mid-1960s, hospital pharmacists, like their colleagues working in the community, were engaged mainly in the compounding and dispensing of medicines. As in community pharmacies, the majority of medicines dispensed from hospital pharmacies are now manufactured by the pharmaceutical industry. Only specialised items, such as certain sterile products which cannot be supplied by industry, are manufactured 'in house'. As the range of drugs available from the pharmaceutical industry increases, and more and more potent drug substances with narrow therapeutic index come onto the market, the potential for serious medication errors, adverse drug reactions and drug interactions has increased.

TABLE 2.1 *Membership of the Pharmaceutical Society by occupation*

Principal Occupation	Number
Community	19 170
Hospital	4 212
Industry	1 375
Wholesale	105
Teaching	386
Other pharmaceutical	583
Non-pharmaceutical	466
No paid employment	4 420
Total	30 717

Adapted from *Pharmaceutical Journal* (1987).

Consequently, the need has arisen for pharmacists to play a more active and direct role in the provision of pharmaceutical services within hospitals. Thus the concept of 'ward pharmacy' has evolved. Pharmacists at the ward level may be involved in patient medication at the pre-prescription stage, working with physicians, supplying them with pharmaceutical and therapeutic information and assisting in the selection of the appropriate medication. In addition to their activities at ward level, hospital pharmacists are now involved in the supply of drugs (to 'in' and 'out' patients), stock control and prescription monitoring. They may also supply drug information to doctors, nurses and other members of the primary health care team, and, where appropriate, to patients and their relatives.

There is scope in the hospital system for a degree of specialisation within hospital pharmacy. Hence pharmacists may specialise in, for example, therapeutic drug monitoring, radio-pharmacy, drug information, production, quality assurance and quality control. 'Community services pharmacists' operate from hospitals and provide a pharmaceutical service to clinics in the community.

2.2 COMMUNITY PHARMACY

The Nuffield Report stated that 'Pharmacists have a unique and vital role to play in the provision of health care to the community'. This Report and the later government White Paper on primary health care (DHSS, 1988) have suggested an extension of the pharmacist's current activities. This expansion of the community pharmacists' role along with the National Pharmaceutical Association's 'Ask your Pharmacist, you'll be taking good advice' campaign, the distribution of health care material by pharmacies through the 'Health care in the high street' (1986) and the 'Pharmacy health care' (1989) schemes, and the advertising of medicines to the public which are only available from pharmacies, has raised the profile of the community pharmacist as a readily accessible provider of health care, and a first port of call in seeking medical advice and treatment.

In Great Britain the number of prescriptions dispensed annually in all pharmacies increased by more than 10 per cent in the ten years up to 1986 (DHSS, 1988), and the average community pharmacy in 1988 dispensed 3000 prescriptions per month (*Pharmaceutical Journal*, 1988a). The main function of the pharmacist, at present then, is the dispensing of prescribed medicines, and seems likely to remain so for the foreseeable future.

Virtually all prescriptions written by general practitioners are dispensed from pharmacies (the remainder, about 5 per cent, being accounted for by dispensing doctors). Pharmacists have an important function in ensuring that patients receive the appropriate medication, that they store it correctly, and are aware of how to take or use it properly. This is particularly important in the light of surveys which have indicated an error rate of between 3 per cent and 5 per cent in prescriptions written by general practitioners (Jones, 1978; Neville *et al.*, 1989). One study monitored the prescriptions generated by eight doctors in a single practice over a period of 3 months (Neville *et al.*, 1989). Of the 15 916 prescriptions generated, 504 (3 per cent) contained some sort of prescribing error. Sixty-two had 'trivial' errors, i.e. were technically incorrect but in which the error was of a very minor nature, or the prescriber's intentions were obvious, for instance spelling errors. A further 273 had 'minor' errors, which involved the pharmacist in making a professional decision but which did not require a consultation with the prescriber, for example ordering an inappropriate pack size of a dermatological product. One hundred and sixty-nine prescriptions had 'major' errors, such that the pharmacist needed to contact the prescriber for clarification, for example if the prescription was illegible or incomplete.

Pharmacists and prescribers share the responsibility for ensuring that the patients receive the appropriate dispensed medicines and are instructed on their correct use – this was highlighted in 1982 by the 'Migril' case, in which it was ruled in the High Court that the pharmacist and the prescriber were equally liable for a prescribed, and subsequently dispensed, overdose of the drug Migril (ergotamine tartrate) which resulted in a patient developing gangrene in both feet (Dale and Appelbe, 1989). In this case the pharmacist who admitted negligence was found to be 45 per cent responsible for the error and the prescriber 55 per cent responsible. In a similar case in which a family suffered side-effects as a result of being prescribed daily instead of weekly doses of the anti-malarial drug chloroquine, the pharmacist and doctor were deemed to be responsible in the ratio of 40:60 respectively (*Pharmaceutical Journal*, 1989b). Consequently it is in the pharmacist's interest, as well as the patient's, that procedures exist and are followed within the pharmacy to ensure that the patient receives the appropriate medication and that the patient will use that medication correctly.

Nowadays, the majority of prescribed medicines dispensed by pharmacists do not need to be formulated from their constituent ingredients. There is also an increasing tendency for medicines manufactured by the pharmaceutical industry to be supplied in packages ready for 'original pack dispensing', whereby a medicine can be supplied to a patient without the pharmacist having to count dosage units. Thus pharmacists are spending less time than in the past in measuring and counting medicines prior to dispensing. The introduction of computers into pharmacies and the availability of appropriate software has also markedly reduced the time spent by pharmacists on activities such as labelling of medicines and stock control.

Taken together these developments have reduced considerably the time required to dispense prescribed medicines. However these developments do not necessarily equate with a lessened role for the pharmacist in the dispensing process. Medicines have become more potent and effective and consequently potentially more dangerous. Therefore it is essential that the patient receives the correct medication and knows how to take it safely. Such a function could not be performed by computer technology, as has been suggested (Roberts, 1988), since computers are fallible, are only as effective as the programmes they run, and are dependent ultimately upon the abilities of the people who operate them. Computers are also unable to make any necessary clinical, professional or pharmaceutical judgements.

The reduction in the time involved in dispensing medicines has created the possibility for pharmacists to develop further their professional activities.

2.3   THE PHARMACIST'S EXTENDED ROLE

A pharmacist's undergraduate and pre-registration training ensures that pharmacists have extensive pharmacological, pharmaceutical and clinical knowledge relating to drug compounds and medicaments. Moreover, pharmacists are required to develop pharmaceutical skills unique among health professionals. These skills enable pharmacists to be more than just dispensers of medicines.

At the point of handing over a dispensed medicine, pharmacists have an opportunity to reiterate and reinforce the prescribers' instructions and, where appropriate, give additional advice and information. By reinforcing the prescriber's instructions, already provided on the medicine's label, pharmacists may facilitate the likelihood of compliance of patients with the prescribed drug regimen. Moreover, since pharmacies are readily accessible in most communities, pharmacists are frequently asked for advice on health care. Such advice may involve the diagnosis and treatment of minor illness and, where necessary, the referral of patients to a general practitioner (see Chapter 9).

In addition, studies of health-centre and community pharmacists have indicated that a majority were being consulted a 'significant' number of times per week by general practitioners and other health professionals, including dentists, midwives, nurses and health visitors (Harding and Taylor, 1988). Some pharmacists then, are recognised as a ready source of drug-related information for other health care professionals as well as to the public.

The increased availability of potent drugs having a narrow therapeutic index, the complex nature of modern drug therapy, and the occurrence of iatrogenic disease ensure that pharmacists, because of their specialist knowledge of drug substances, have a crucial contribution to make to primary health care. The change in the nature of dispensing has also allowed pharmacists to begin developing other aspects of their professional activities. Moreover the public is increasingly exercising its power as the consumer of health care resources and services. The public's expectations of health care professionals has risen; therefore these professions must be prepared to offer a high quality service and, if required, a competitive range of services. The services offered by pharmacists in addition to the traditional dispensing activities have become known as pharmacists' 'extended role'. The government's Green and White Papers on primary health care (DHSS, 1986, 1988), which built on the findings and recommendations of the earlier Nuffield Inquiry, outlined some of the features of the 'extended role' of the pharmacist, and determined the likely future development of pharmaceutical services. The 'extended role' as such has not actually been comprehensively defined; however, Table 2.2 indicates those components which have been suggested by the

Nuffield Inquiry, and the government's Green and White papers. Other features may be added in due course.

Advising patients on minor ailments, recommending treatments and 'counselling' patients on the correct way to use purchased or prescribed medication form the major elements of the 'extended role'.

Studies of the British public's health have indicated that 90 per cent of individuals suffer from at least one minor ailment within a two-week period (British Market Research Bureau, 1987). Pharmacists in the community are uniquely placed to advise patients on the most appropriate and effective way of dealing with such ailments. Pharmacies are visited daily by an estimated six million people (*Pharmaceutical Journal*, 1988b), including those who are healthy as well as those who are ill. Pharmacists are unique amongst health professionals in that they are readily available to the public, and can be consulted without the necessity of a prior appointment. Pharmacists are therefore able both to advise on matters of health care, and provide treatment when necessary. Health care advice may be provided by the pharmacist through personal consultation and/or by the provision of educational literature. This aspect of the pharmacist's activities is discussed further in chapter nine.

TABLE 2.2   *The pharmacist's 'extended role'*

1. Advise patients on minor ailments.
2. Advise patients on sensible and effective ways of using medicines.
3. Provision of domiciliary services to housebound/isolated patients.
4. Participation in continuing education of community health care practitioners.
5. Health education and promotion.
6. Supervision of supply and safekeeping of medicines in residential homes.
7. Keep records of prescribed and purchased medication.
8. Registration of elderly patients.
9. Advise prescribers on economic and effective prescribing and on the effects of medicines.
10. Monitoring and reporting adverse drug reactions and interactions.
11. Advising general practitioners on the administration and handling of complex substances.
12. Diagnostic testing, e.g. measurement of blood pressure and blood glucose and cholesterol levels.

Other aspects of the 'extended role' depend on the pharmacist having a more active input into the delivery of primary health care. Pharmacists are participating more directly in the education of community health workers, such as those in residential homes for children, the handicapped and the elderly. Moreover, they are increasingly encouraged to assist in the supervision of supply and safekeeping of the medicines in these institutions. Pharmacists may serve as a bridge between prescribers and community health workers, thereby enhancing the care of people in these establishments (*Pharmaceutical Journal*, 1988c; Lapsley, 1988). Pharmacists have also been encouraged to keep medication records of elderly and confused patients (DHSS, 1988). Such records, it is argued, will allow pharmacists to accurately monitor the medication of such patients, enabling them to rapidly identify potential drug interactions or contra-indications.

One of the obstacles to pharmacists taking up the challenges presented by the 'extended role' may be the way in which the Chemist Contractors of the National Health Service are remunerated. The current system provides payment to Contractors almost exclusively on the basis of prescribed items supplied to patients. This remuneration procedure offers little, if any, financial incentive for pharmacists to be involved in other activities such as advising patients, health promotion, or the maintenance of patient medication records. It has been suggested, too, that there be a relaxation in the rules governing the supervision of dispensing by pharmacists, thus allowing pharmacists the time to perform additional functions. This suggestion has proved to be a highly sensitive issue, causing acrimonious debate within the pharmacy profession, and culminating in a special general meeting of the Royal Pharmaceutical Society of Great Britain, in which a motion opposing the Society's council's proposals for such a relaxation was passed (Royal Pharmaceutical Society, 1989).

Currently, then, the way the pharmaceutical profession can best implement the 'extended role' is still being debated. What is certain, however, is that the role of the pharmacist has changed considerably in recent years, and will continue to change. As pharmacists become increasingly involved in new activities and have a greater input into primary health care, they have to acquire new knowledge and develop new skills if their input is to be significant and if they are to remain at all credible in the eyes of other health professionals and the consumer of their services – the public.

References

British Market Research Bureau Ltd. (1987) *Everyday Health Care, a Consumer Study of Self-Medication in Great Britain*, London, The Proprietary Association of Great Britain.

Dale, J. R. and Appelbe, G. E. (1989) *Pharmacy Law and Ethics*, London, Pharmaceutical Press.

DHSS (1986) *Primary Health Care: An Agenda for Discussion* (Cmd 9771), London, HMSO.

DHSS (1988) *Promoting Better Health*, (Cmd 249), London, HMSO.

Elworthy, P. H. (1986) The Pattern of Women Pharmacists, 1966 to 1983, *Pharmaceutical Journal*, 237: 218-224.

Harding, G. and Taylor, K.M.G. (1988) Pharmacies in Health Centres, *Journal of the Royal College of General Practitioners*, 38: 566-567.

Jones, D. R. (1978) Errors on Doctors' Prescriptions, *Journal of the Royal College of General Practitioners*, 28: 543-545.

Lapsley, R. (1988) Prescription Monitoring in a Nursing Home, *Pharmaceutical Journal*, 240: 688.

Neville, R. G., Robertson, F., Livingston, S. and Crombie, I. K. (1989) A Classification of Prescription Errors, *Journal of the Royal College of General Practitioners*, 39: 110-112.

Nuffield Committee of Inquiry into Pharmacy (1986) *Pharmacy: a report to the Nuffield foundation*, London, Nuffield Foundation.

Pharmaceutical Journal (1987) Survey of Pharmacists, 238: 685.

Pharmaceutical Journal (1988a) '3000 Average', 240: 175.

Pharmaceutical Journal (1988b) Six Million Chances Daily for Health Education, 241: 179.

Pharmaceutical Journal (1988c) Residential Home Staff need help from Pharmacist, Study Finds, 40: 217.

Pharmaceutical Journal (1989b) Pharmacist Liable for Doctor's Error, 243: 186.

Roberts, D. (1988) Dispensing by the Community Pharmacist: an Unstoppable Decline? *Journal of the Royal College of General Practitioners*, 38: 563-564.

Royal Pharmaceutical Society (1989) Narrow but Clear Majority for no Confidence Motion, *Pharmaceutical Journal*, 242: 438.

Stone, P. and Curtis, S. J. (1989) *Pharmacy Practice*, London, Farrand Press.

3 Sociological Understanding of Health and Illness

This chapter examines the way in which individuals experience and exhibit symptoms, and explores the factors that influence their responses to symptoms. It also illustrates that patients' experience of symptoms does not inevitably lead to their seeking help from a health care professional. The way in which people respond to symptoms is often more complex than might at first be imagined. For instance, it may be assumed that a simple correlation exists between the severity of symptoms and the decision to consult a health professional.

In other words, we might assume that the worse the patient feels the more likely they are to seek professional health care. In reality, the utilisation of health services is influenced by a wide range of factors which sometimes overrides the severity of the symptoms. Many of these factors have been identified and studied since the inception of the National Health Service in 1948.

Much of the thinking behind the policies which led to the foundation of the National Health Service in the 1940s rested on the premiss that people who experience symptoms of ill-health would seek medical aid if the services were free at the point of use and readily available. Moreover, it was believed that after the creation of a universally free service there would be a dramatic rise in the demand for medical care, but that once the backlog of ill-health in the community had been treated, this demand would stabilise and the need and demand for such services would, in time, become more stable.

The reality however did not match this apparent logic. Indeed this misinterpretation was due to a lack of awareness and understanding about the nature and prevalence of health and illness in the community.

3.1   ILLNESS AS A SOCIAL CONCEPT

In order to understand how patients respond to ill-health it is useful to appreciate the differences between illness and disease. Disease refers to a pathological or biological condition, for example cancer of the lung or kidney failure. Illness, on the other hand, concerns individuals' responses to symptoms: how they feel, experience and make sense of their sickness. Illness and disease are not therefore synonymous – it is possible to feel ill without suffering a disease and to suffer a disease without feeling ill. For instance, a woman who has cervical cancer may feel perfectly healthy, whilst someone who is ill through excessive stress may not exhibit a pathological disease. The distinction between illness and disease is important because it emphasises the fact that the way in which people respond to symptoms is often as important as the disease state itself. Nevertheless this distinction can be misleading because disease itself is not unequivocal. Pathological norms have changed over time and are not universally accepted. Comparative studies indicate that what counts as disease in one setting may be considered normal in another. For example, one study describes how amongst some South American tribes the skin disease referred to as dichromic spirochetosis within western medicine, is so common that those who do not have the condition are regarded as abnormal. Those that do not exhibit the features of the 'disease' might even be excluded from marriage (Ackernecht, 1947).

The boundary between sickness and health is not clear cut. Illness is a variance from normality, and what is 'normal' varies between societies, cultures, and groups within society. In this sense illness is a socially defined concept – that is, the implicit meaning of illness is not universally shared but is peculiar to specific cultures and societies.

3.2   FREQUENCY OF SYMPTOMS: THE SYMPTOM ICEBERG

Today we realise that the majority of symptoms experienced by people are not presented to a health professional. The majority of individuals either fail to perceive their symptoms, or ignore, tolerate or self-treat them. The fact that the majority of symptoms

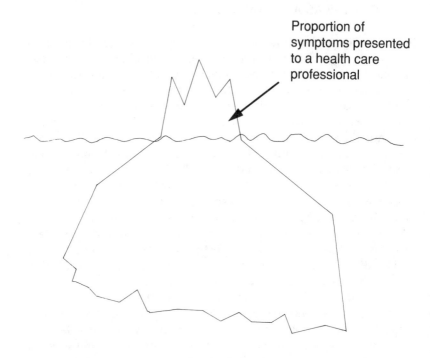

Proportion of
symptoms presented
to a health care
professional

FIGURE 3.1   *Frequency of symptoms: the symptom iceberg*

are not presented to a health professional has been referred to
by Hannay (1979) as the 'symptom iceberg'. This is represented
diagrammatically in Figure 3.1.

Surveys of the general population have shown that symptoms
are frequently experienced by most adults. Evidence of the frequent experience of symptoms was reported in a study of women
aged 16–44 years (Scambler *et al.*, 1981). These women were asked
to keep a diary of any occurrence of illness. Symptoms were
recorded on average one day in three, but only one medical consultation was sought for every eighteen recorded symptoms.

Further evidence of the frequent experience of symptoms was
found in a study of the incidence of illness amongst over one thousand adults in Great Britain. This study found that over 95 per cent
of these adults reported experiencing at least one symptom/illness
during two-week and twelve-month periods (Table 3.1). These
ailments included some which were seasonal, some which were
chronic and others which were recurrent in nature. In response

to these ailments, 45 per cent of the respondents took no action at all. Thirty-six percent used an Over The Counter (OTC) medicine or home remedy, whilst only 13 per cent saw a doctor or dentist (Table 3.2).

Thus whilst the range and incidence of symptoms in the population as a whole has been found to be very high, the proportion of people who actively seek professional help in response to these symptoms is low. These findings correspond well with those of earlier studies. For instance, Wadsworth *et al.* (1971) in a study of the incidence of symptoms over two weeks in two London boroughs found that of a thousand randomly selected individuals, 19 per cent experienced symptoms but took no action, 56 per cent who experienced symptoms took some form of self-medication, 17 per cent did consult with a general practitioner, whilst 3 per cent were outpatients and 0.5 per cent were inpatients in hospital. Only 5 per cent reported experiencing no symptoms at all. Not only does the presence of a symptom not necessarily precipitate a consultation with a health professional, but there is also evidence that deciding whether or not to visit a health professional does not simply depend on the severity of the symptom itself. For example, it has been found that patients who suffered from severe facial pain did not seek professional treatment (Marbach and Lipton, 1978).

The existence of a 'symptom iceberg' has significant implications for health care delivery in general, and pharmaceutical service

TABLE 3.1 *Incidence of reported illness
over a two-week and twelve-month period (n=1217)*

	Percentage of adults experiencing illness	
	2 weeks	12 months
Tiredness	35	57
Common cold	15	66
Sleeping disturbance	15	26
Arthritis/rheumatism	12	21
Nausea/sickness	5	22
Diarrhoea	4	19
Influenza/virus	3	30
Hay fever	2	10

Adapted from British Market Research Bureau Ltd (1987).

delivery in particular. These studies have revealed that there is a reservoir of untreated symptoms and ailments within the community, some of which could be dealt with effectively by the pharmacist. For example, seemingly 'minor' ailments such as sinusitis, hay fever and the common cold could be evaluated by the pharmacist as to whether or not they warranted the attention of a general practitioner, a specialist clinic, or a dentist.

The pharmacist is ideally positioned to contribute substantially towards meeting this potential demand, for which existing services would appear to be inappropriate or inadequate. Many general practitioners complain that they are frequently consulted for what they consider to be 'trivial conditions'. In one national study it was reported that a quarter of the general practitioners questioned felt that half or more of their surgery consultations fell into this category (Cartwright and Anderson, 1981). Many conditions could be more suitably dealt with by community pharmacists. It is nevertheless important to appreciate that whilst complaints may be considered trivial by a general practitioner, they may be very significant to the patient.

Medical sociologists have explored the puzzle, highlighted by the 'symptom iceberg', that although people experience ill-health they frequently do not seek professional help. The findings from these studies have proved to be valuable in terms of understanding the processes involved in becoming ill and the actions taken by people in response to their illness.

Figure 3.2 illustrates that a range of factors come into play before a patient might ultimately consult with a health professional. At

TABLE 3.2 *The response of adults to minor ailments*

Saw doctor/dentist	13%
Used prescription medicine already in the house	13%
Bought an OTC medicine	11%
Used an OTC medicine already in the house	16%
Used a 'home remedy'	9%
Did not use anything	45%
Don't know/not stated	7%

Adapted from British Market Research Bureau Ltd (1987).

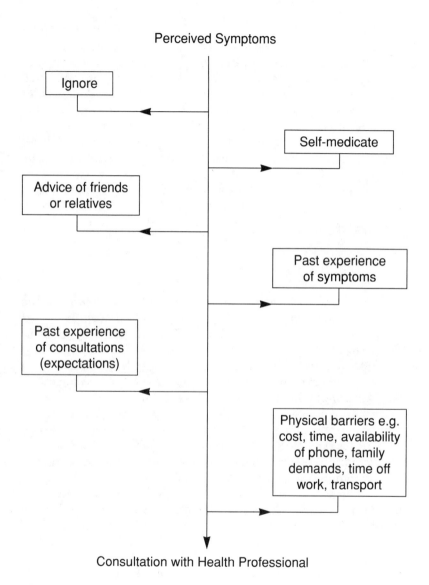

FIGURE 3.2 *Consultation as a social process*

any point in the continuum other considerations, such as a previously unpleasant experience with a dentist, general practitioner
or other health professional, a particularly busy period at work, or
simply having no ready access to a telephone or transport, may
dissuade patients from seeking professional health care. When all
factors are considered, the 'costs' may outweigh the 'benefits' of
seeking help or advice. This cost/benefit approach to analysing the
use of health services was found to be instructive in understanding
people's actions in relation to the use of health services (Le Grand,
1982). Clearly the perceived costs and benefits are influenced by
an individual's material resources (see Chapter 6). When costs
outweigh the benefits, people may tend to either self-medicate or
allow their symptoms to remain untreated.

3.3 ILLNESS BEHAVIOUR

The presence of symptoms alone, then, does not determine the
use of health services. Instead, uptake of these services is to a
large extent determined by how individuals respond to these
symptoms.

The study of 'illness behaviour' is the study of behaviour in
its social context, rather than in relation to a physiological or
pathological condition. Being sick can be regarded as an active
process, not a passive state, that is to say, being ill involves the
individual (and others) in interpreting their symptoms, choosing
what to do about their experience of illness or sickness, and
finally deciding what course of action to take in response to
the symptoms – to attempt to alleviate them or to simply ignore
them. 'Illness behaviour' is a sociological concept which describes
how people respond to their symptoms. This implies that the way
in which symptoms are perceived, evaluated and acted upon is
influenced by people's previous health-related experiences and an
individual's social environment.

Two perspectives on illness behaviour have been identified and
termed 'individualistic' and 'collectivist' approaches (Morgan *et al.*,
1985). The former approach stresses the characteristics of the individual, whilst the latter emphasises the shared social norms and
values that influence the actions of people within social groups.

Mechanic (1968) has identified ten variables which may influence the individual's response to illness.

1. Visibility, recognisability, or perceived importance of deviant signs and symptoms.
2. The extent to which a person's symptoms are perceived as serious. (That is, the person's estimate of the present and future probability of danger indicated by these symptoms.)
3. The extent to which symptoms disrupt family life, work and other social activities.
4. The frequency of the appearance of the deviant signs and symptoms, their persistence, or the frequency of their recurrence.
5. The tolerance threshold of those who are exposed to and evaluate the deviant signs and symptoms.
6. Available information, knowledge and cultural assumptions and understandings of the evaluator.
7. Psychological factors that lead to denial of symptoms; for example, fear of confirmation of disease such as cancer.
8. More pressing or immediate needs may compete with illness responses; for example, work commitments may be regarded as more important than dealing with illness.
9. Competing possible interpretations that can be assigned to the symptoms once they are recognised.
10. Availability of treatment resources, physical proximity, and psychological and monetary costs of taking action (included are not only physical distance and costs of time, money and effort, but also such costs as social stigma, social distance and feelings of humiliation).

These factors are undoubtedly relevant considerations which influence an individual's response to illness. Collectivist modes of approach point out that illness behaviour is a culturally learned response, in other words the experience of illness is defined according to the prevailing norms and values of a society or community. It is not the symptoms themselves that are significant in comprehending illness behaviour, but the way in which the symptoms are defined and interpreted. Symptoms which are considered to be normal in one context may be considered to be abnormal in another.

This 'normalising' process is a common and frequent part of everyday life. However when symptoms prevent a person from behaving 'normally', as expected by themselves or others, then the symptoms may no longer be considered 'normal'. In this event a search for explanations to make sense of the symptom may ensue. For example, whether two individuals with a persistent cough experience this symptom in the same way will depend on a number of social factors. So a person living in a damp house may interpret their early morning hacking cough, not as something out of the ordinary, but as 'normal'; an everyday experience shared by neighbours, which does not require presentation to a health care professional (Holland and Walker, 1971). A person living in a centrally-heated house with a similar cough might perceive this symptom quite differently – as a symptom of possible serious illness requiring urgent professional health care.

People therefore evaluate their physical and/or emotional sensations in terms of their existing knowledge, experience and advice from other people. Hence when we talk of illness behaviour we are saying that responses to symptoms are learned in accordance with the individual's social environment. Koos (1954) illustrated that although lower back pain is quite a common condition among lower-class women, it is not considered symptomatic of any disease or disorder, but rather part of their everyday existence. For women having more favourable socio-economic circumstances, the onset of back pain was more likely to result in a visit to a general practitioner.

Within any social environment there may be different cultures. Cultural differences may be significant in determining how individuals interpret and respond to their symptoms. It has also been pointed out that it is possible to identify responses to illness which are common to groups of individuals. Zola, for example, in a study of North Americans of Irish and Italian decent, found a direct link between the membership of a cultural group and the communication of bodily complaints. Their response to illness reflected their responses to their other troubles and problems. The Irish Americans responded to their symptoms by denial of their sickness, whilst the Italians responded by dramatisation (Zola, 1966). A similar study conducted in New York (Zborowski, 1952), found that patients of Old-American or Irish origin displayed a pragmatic attitude towards pain and, when it was particularly intense, they showed a tendency to withdraw from the company of others. By contrast, individuals of Italian or Jewish background tended to be more demanding and dependent as patients and were inclined to seek sympathy.

More recently, Morgan and Watkins (1988) explored the perceptions and responses of 62 European 'white' and West Indian hypertensive patients. Although both groups of patients were aware of the importance of controlling their blood pressure, and all identified stress as a causal factor, they differed in their attitude to anti-hypertensive medication. Almost all (26 out of 30) of the 'white' respondents said they took the tablets as prescribed, compared with only 12 of the 30 West Indian respondents. The 'leaving off' of drugs by the West Indian patients was explained by their concern about the long term side-effects of drug use and their dislike of being dependent on medication. Some of these patients also questioned the need to take drugs if they felt all right. Moreover, the partial rejection of long term drug therapy by this group was associated with the use of herbal remedies taken as well as or as an alternative to their prescribed medication.

We have shown that the way in which people experience and respond to symptoms is a complex process. The 'illness experience' should not be considered in isolation from the person's social and cultural context. In the following chapter we shall consider further the importance of an individual's social environment in shaping their experience of health and illness.

Further Reading

Black, N. *et al.* (1984) *Health and Disease*, Milton Keynes, Open University Press. Part One and Part Six.

Currer, C. and Stacey, M. (eds.) (1986) *Concepts of Health, Illness and Disease: A Comparative Perspective*, Lemington Spa, Berg Publications Ltd.

Fitzpatrick, R. *et al.* (1984) *The Experience of Illness*, London, Tavistock. Chapter Three.

Hannay, R. (1979) *The Symptom Iceberg: a Study of Community Health*, London, Routledge and Kegan Paul.

References

Ackernecht, E. W. (1947) The Role of Medical History in Medical Examination, *Bulletin of the History of Medicine, 21*

British Market Research Bureau Ltd. (1987) *Everyday Health Care, a Consumer Study of Self-Medication in Great Britain*, London, The Proprietary Association of Great Britain.

26   *Sociology for Pharmacists*

Cartwright, A. and Anderson, R. (1981) *General Practice Revisited: a Second Study of Patients and their Doctors*, London, Tavistock Publications.

Hannay, R. (1979) *The Symptom Iceberg: a Study in Community Health*, London, Routledge and Kegan Paul.

Holland, W. W. and Walker, J. (1971) Population Studies in the London Borough of Lambeth, *Community Medicine*, 126, 153.

Koos, E. (1954) *The Health of Regionsville: What the People Felt and Did About It*, New York, Columbia University Press.

Le Grand, J. (1982) *The Strategy of Equality*, London, Allen Unwin.

Marbach, J. J. and Lipton, J. A. (1978) Aspects of Illness Behaviour in Patients with Facial Pain, *Journal of the American Dental Association*, 96: 630–638.

Mechanic, D. (1968) *Medical Sociology: A Selective View*, New York, Free Press.

Morgan, M., Calnan, M. and Manning, N. (1985) *Sociological Approaches to Health and Medicine*, London, Routledge and Kegan Paul.

Morgan, M. and Watkins, C. J. (1988) Managing Hypertension Beliefs and Responses to Medication among cultural groups, *Sociology of Health and Illness*, 10: 561–578.

Scambler, A., Scambler, G. and Craig, D. (1981) Kinship and Friendship Networks and Women's Demands for Primary Care, *Journal of the Royal College of General Practitioners*, 26: 746–750.

Wadsworth, M., Butterfield, W. and Blaney, R. (1971) *Health and Sickness: The Choice of Treatment*, London, Tavistock Publications.

Zborowski, M. (1952) Cultural components in response to pain, *Journal of Social Issues*, 8: 16–30.

Zola, I. K. (1966) Culture and Symptoms, an analysis of patients presenting complaints, *American Sociological Review*, 31: 615–630.

4 Lay Health Beliefs and 'Help-Seeking' Behaviour

In 1983 the National Pharmaceutical Association (NPA) introduced a campaign to raise the profile of the pharmacist in the community. The 'Ask your pharmacist, you'll be taking good advice' campaign was designed to encourage the public to consult their pharmacist for health advice and for the treatment of minor symptoms. The decision-making process leading to people seeking professional health care or advice, as we have seen in chapter three, is not 'triggered' simply by the onset or the severity of symptoms. What is more significant is how the symptoms are perceived and interpreted. Furthermore, actions taken in response to symptoms are mediated by other factors such as the 'costs' and 'benefits' of seeking help, and the responses of friends, colleagues and relatives, to an individual's illness.

4.1 INITIATING A CONSULTATION WITH A HEALTH CARE PROFESSIONAL

Deciding when, or indeed whether or not, to use health care services, is influenced by the composition of one's immediate network of family and friends, their values and their attitude to professional health care. Irvine Zola, an American medical sociologist, has established five types of responses whereby a symptom may be experienced by a patient as being abnormal, thereby triggering the individual to seek health care advice. Zola (1973) identified these triggers as:

1. *Perceived interference with vocational or physical activity.*
   If the experience of a symptom or symptoms begins to interfere with one's routine ability to work or to take part in routine physical activities, then the symptom(s) may be regarded as 'abnormal'.

2. *Perceived interference with social or personal relations.*
    Cause for concern may arise when the experience of
    symptoms interferes with one's normal patterns of social
    interaction. Of course what is considered normal will differ
    from individual to individual, depending on such factors as
    occupation, lifestyle, age and so forth.

3. *The occurrence of interpersonal crisis.*
    During periods of stable and harmonious interpersonal rela-
    tionships, common and trivial symptoms may be regarded as
    inoffensive. The breakdown of such relationships, however,
    can have profound effects on the way symptoms are experi-
    enced. Symptoms that were previously barely perceived,
    might, in the course of an interpersonal crisis, suddenly
    be discerned as a threat to health. Interpersonal crises can
    also diminish people's ability to cope with long-standing
    symptoms. Strategies for coping with a chronic pain can be
    undermined by interpersonal crises, and result in enhancing
    the perception of that pain.

4. *Temporalising symptoms.*
    Another trigger may be the persistence of a symptom which
    may or may not interfere with work or personal relations,
    nonetheless remaining a source of concern or puzzlement to
    an individual. This may lead the person to decide to give the
    symptom a set number of days or weeks during which time
    to abate. In the event of the symptom not abating during this
    time, then the individual may seek professional help. This is
    exemplified by statements such as 'Oh, if it's not better by
    Monday I'll do something about it'.

5. *Sanctioning.*
    While the person experiencing the symptoms may feel they
    do not warrant professional attention, perceiving them as
    either trivial or unimportant, pressure exerted by family or
    friends may lead to a visit to a health care professional.
    Similarly, the symptom may be a cause of anxiety to the
    sufferer but they may choose to avoid seeking professional
    help for fear that their complaint may be considered trivial.
    Confirmation from family or friends that they have a legiti-
    mate claim for professional help may trigger the sufferer to
    take appropriate action.

We can see from Zola's triggers that it is not simply a question of being or not being conscious of symptoms nor of their severity which necessarily determines what is to be done about them. The role of friends, families and colleagues is also a major factor in this process.

4.2   LAY REFERRAL SYSTEMS

The decision to act upon symptoms is not necessarily taken exclusively by the sufferer, but is often the result of discussions with a range of people: immediate members of a patient's family, their friends or colleagues. Freidson (1970) refers to this network of friends, relatives and colleagues as the 'lay referral system'. The decision to use or avoid professional health care services, Freidson maintains, is influenced by (a) the extent of 'close knit social relations' within the members who make up a person's lay referral system and (b) the predominant values and attitudes to professional health care within that lay referral system. For example, whether or not a person lives in an extended family, in which individuals have daily or frequent contact with a range of relatives such as parents, grandparents, aunts and uncles; or the extent to which ideas of health and illness do or do not match those of health professionals; or whether or not people live relatively independent of others, each may play a part in influencing an individual's decision to seek professional health care.

Table 4.1 indicates that those people whose conceptions of health and illness are compatible with those of health professionals and who live within close-knit communities are most likely to use professional services. Conversely, those people living in close-knit communities whose conceptions of health and illness differ from those of health professionals are least likely to use services. In transient communities, that is, communities whose members are constantly changing, where conceptions of health and illness are congruent with official notions of health, there is still a high degree of utilisation, but it is noticeably lower in such communities where people's conceptions are at odds with those of health care practitioners. An example of the lay referral system as proposed by Freidson was found in a study of the use of maternity services by working-class mothers in Aberdeen (McKinlay, 1973). Those

TABLE 4.1   *Uptake of health services
as influenced by the lay referral system*

Lay Referral Structure	Lay Culture	
	Compatible with Profession	Incompatible with Profession
Transitory	Medium to high use of services	Medium to low use of services
Stable	Highest use of services	Lowest use of services

Adapted from Freidson (1970).

mothers who had relatives living close by and who visited friends infrequently were found to be under-utilisers of health care services, whereas those mothers who lived more closely to friends rather than relatives, and who had more friends of their own age were found to be service utilisers. This latter group were found to make considerable use of friends and husbands and consulted less with their mothers and other relatives on matters of health. Moreover they consulted with a narrow range of lay persons. In other words, women with immediate family ties consulted less with the health care services than women who were more reliant on friends. A person's immediate social environment, the composition of family and friendship networks, then, can play a significant role in determining the frequency with which health professionals will be consulted.

4.3   LAY HEALTH CARE WORKERS

We can all be considered 'health workers' in as much as we may, at some time or another, be responsible for the health of ourselves and for others.

The idea that we may be involved in the provision of health care is easier to appreciate if we consider a broader notion of health care than has hitherto been the norm. For example, self-care such as cleaning our teeth, eating a healthy diet and taking exercise, can be conceived of as health care. Looking after family and friends is also an important aspect of health care. Indeed, such informal carers, the majority of whom are unpaid, comprise a very significant proportion of health workers in our society.

Stacey has argued in her book, *The Sociology of Health and Healing* (1988), that

1. All members of society are actively involved in health production and maintenance work.
2. Everyone is potentially involved in health work as a patient, and that the patient is a health worker.
3. More people than the officially recognised healers are health workers.
4. The characteristics of 'human service' or 'people work' involved in health work, result in the activity having characteristics which distinguish it from most other social activities.

In addition to traditional health care workers, such as general practitioners, dentists and nurses, the community pharmacist is also in constant communication with other health workers including people who are practising self-care, and parents, friends and relatives who are caring for others. Our society depends on these workers or unpaid carers and they have been referred to as the 'hidden labour of the NHS' (Taylor, 1979). The changing demographic structure of our society, and the fact that increasing numbers of people are living beyond 65 years of age has not been matched by a corresponding increase in the funding for the provision of care to the community. This has led to a growing dependency on the family and friends for the care of elderly relatives (Allen, 1985).

4.4 LAY HEALTH BELIEFS

It has been suggested that there must be a relationship between health beliefs and behaviour. Attempts to understand this relationship can be divided into socio-psychological approaches and sociological approaches. A characteristic of the former has been the attempts to construct models which can be used to explain and describe the impact that health beliefs have on health behaviours. One such model is the Health Belief Model (HBM) (Rosenstock, 1966; Becker, 1974). The HBM attempts to identify motives which influence people's health-related actions and tries to recognise those which are most vulnerable to change. Factors such as age and sex would be immutable; subjective factors in the form of people's perceptions would be alterable. The factors in the health belief model are: the level of interest an individual expresses in health issues (health motivation); their perceived vulnerability to illness (susceptibility); the perceived seriousness of certain illnesses (severity); and the perceived value of taking health actions (benefits and costs). An assessment of these perceptions, it is argued, will enable the researcher or health educator to identify the likelihood and willingness of the individual to comply with 'desirable' health behaviours.

This argument is particularly attractive to health educators because if it is possible to identify ways in which behaviour can be changed, they could act upon and advise those who do not subscribe to healthy actions. However, social reality is not so straightforward. The Health Belief Model assumes that if individuals have the appropriate motives and perceptions, they will undertake professionally prescribed health routines and actions. It thus underestimates the wider social constraints and circumstances in which people live. It also takes as given the value of professionally defined actions, and as a corollary underplays alternative non-professional health-related actions.

Studies which have attempted to evaluate the HBM have found that the level of variance in behaviour as a function of health belief/motivational variables is small and thus the predictive value of the model is negligible (Calnan, 1984). This highlights as problematic a fundamental assumption on which the HBM is based, that is, to what extent can we assume a correlative relation between belief and behaviour.

As we have seen people's responses to symptoms are many, varied and diverse. People's ideas and beliefs about health are derived from many sources and have also been the subject of study by medical sociologists. The first sociological studies of people's views of health and illness appeared in the early 1960s (Apple, 1960; Freidson, 1961). This interest in what people think and have to say about health and illness has resulted in a variety of studies in which the ideas and beliefs of people have been defined and analysed. The ideas of individuals with regard to health and illness are referred to in the sociological literature as 'lay health beliefs'. Understanding lay health beliefs is useful and important because they serve to:

1. Enhance our understanding of the social impact and meaning of health, disease, and illness.
2. Enhance the health professional-patient relationship.
3. Allow the development of realistic approaches and strategies in health education and promotion.
4. Allow the development of appropriate health services based on the perceived needs of sufferers rather than simply on the perceptions of health care providers.

Using qualitative research methods (described in Chapter 10), a number of medical sociologists have researched the form and content of lay beliefs about health and illness in western communities. A significant finding from this work is the confirmation that lay ideas concerning health are not simply crude distortions of medical knowledge, but often display their own logic, coherence and sophistication (Blaxter, 1983). To explore this contention more fully, let us consider two characteristics of lay views that have emerged from the literature: first the experiential or biographical quality, and second the multiplicity of ideas held by any one individual about disease and illness.

Experiential/biographical model

The biographical quality of people's views was identified and developed by Williams and Wood (1986) in their research on people who suffered from arthritis. They revealed that patients have a genuine and urgent interest in understanding why they have the disease, and develop 'models' in order to explain and make sense of it. The sufferers also had additional purposes which played an important part in determining the choice of their beliefs; these included the need to locate etiological explanations within their own life experiences.

An example quoted by Williams and Wood concerned a man who explained his rheumatoid arthritis as being a direct result of specific life experiences which included stress incurred during the war, when he had worked in a bomb disposal unit, and also his long term exposure to the natural elements when he was employed on a building site. All these events were regarded by the sufferer as important contributory factors to his disease: but it was after a post-operative infection that he felt his arthritis had really 'gone to town'.

Similarly, in a study of views about disease, Blaxter (1983) found that the forty-six women interviewed developed causal models to explain their bouts of illness, displaying a high degree of sophistication. Social factors were recognised as mediating between an ultimate cause and the onset of illness. For example, influenza was believed to be caused by a virus, but factors such as general susceptibility to such an illness, feeling run down and/or getting wet (for example being caught in a storm), all entered into their explanations. Thus, whilst these women acknowledged the bio-medical cause of the illness, this was interpreted in the light of their life experiences.

Multiplicity of ideas model

A second finding of sociological studies of lay health beliefs is the prevalence of a multiplicity of ideas that may be held by any one individual. In a study of patients' beliefs about hypertension, for example, Blumhagen (1980) found ten different kinds of causal factors which were commonly cited by sufferers. These included chronic external stress, genetic make-up, salt and water intake. Blumhagen further found that some respondents gave unrelated explanations for the cause of their hypertension at different stages of the interview. It is interesting to note that, when confronted by these differing explanations, the patients did not feel that they presented problems or were in any way inconsistent. Each explanation was derived from differing sources and within its context made sense. To describe this quality of lay health beliefs, Fitzpatrick *et al.* (1984) have referred to them as 'syncretic,' by which they mean that 'ideas are drawn selectively from a variety of different traditions and adjusted according to the current concerns of the individual'.

Comparative studies of lay beliefs about the aetiology of illness have helped us to appreciate that people's ideas and beliefs, which at first may appear strange, do contain their own rationale and logic. It is evident that the search for an explanation of the cause of illness is important to people who experience that illness. Chrisman (1977) in a review of the literature from different cultures on lay ideas about aetiology identified four commonly used explanations to account for the pathology of the body in the event of ill-health.

1.　Invasion: the rationale that the body is susceptible to intrusion of matter or substances that are able to make the body ill, such as micro-organisms, toxic chemicals, or spoiled food.

2. Degeneration: whereby the body is perceived and expected to get progressively worse with age.
3. Mechanical: the structure or functioning of the body is impeded as the result of blockages, fractures, breakdowns, and similar occurrences.
4. Balance: the imperative of maintaining an equilibrium between elements within the body and between the body and the environment.

People's lay health beliefs are particularly relevant in relation to so-called 'behavioural diseases' such as Acquired Immune Deficiency Syndrome (AIDS). In a study of 'Young People's Health Beliefs and AIDS', Warwick *et al.* (1988) stress three reasons why young people's views are important: (a) lay beliefs may temper the effectiveness of the official health education messages which rely on professional and bio-medical explanations to inform people about the causes of the AIDS virus; (b) people's ideas and beliefs are likely to influence their perception of 'risks'; (c) lay beliefs have an impact on the way disease is understood and interpreted, and thus experienced. The researchers discussed with young people who were attending community-based youth groups and youth training programmes their ideas about Human Immunodeficiency Virus (HIV) infection and AIDS. They found that these young people had various levels of awareness and a varied knowledge. For example, whether or not one contracts an HIV infection or develops 'full blown' AIDS was often believed to be a matter of chance or bad luck and was based on the notion that 'the virus' or 'the actual AIDS' was easily transmitted. The issue of AIDS in relation to health education and the pharmacist is discussed further in chapter nine.

4.5   THE SICK ROLE

In the preceding chapter we suggested that what constitutes 'normality' is socially specific. In other words, what is considered normal varies between societies and between groups within society. Following from this appreciation, illness has been conceived by some sociologists as a 'deviant' state, in that to be ill implies a departure from normality. The notion of illness as deviance developed in the 1950s out of critiques of the bio-medical model of illness, which explained illness behaviour purely as a breakdown of the normal functioning of the body.

The work of an American sociologist, Talcott Parsons, figures largely among these critiques. Parsons (1951) defined illness not as a biological state but as a social role – namely the 'sick role'. This role distinguishes those who are healthy from those whom society, and the medical profession in particular, classify as being sick. The purpose of this distinction, Parsons argues, is to ensure the cohesion of society. In playing out our everyday conventional roles, for example as employees or employers, as unemployed, as members of families, or as pensioners, the social order is maintained: employment creates earnings and wealth, families are supported by parents and/or the state and so on. These roles, he suggests, have a positive and purposeful function in maintaining the social order. Taking on roles which are not conventional, for example that of a criminal or 'drop out', undermines the social order and is generally considered deviant behaviour because conventional roles are not being filled.

The 'sick role' maintains the cohesion of society since those who are incapacitated are given the privilege of having their conventional day-to-day responsibilities and duties suspended in order to allow them to restore themselves to health and expedite their return to the social system, with its obligations, duties and roles.

In Western society only a medical practitioner can legitimise entry into the sick role. Once admitted to this role, the patient gains two benefits:

1. Patients are temporarily excused their normal roles. Gaining a sickness certificate from the doctor is the obvious way in which this expectation is met. Merely visiting the doctor, however, confers some legitimacy on the claim to be sick. Whereas 'feeling unwell' might be treated sceptically by friends and colleagues, a visit to the doctor may be sufficient to gain credibility.
2. Patients are not held responsible for their illness. Not being held responsible for the illness relieves the patient of a considerable burden in our society. In some other societies the patient may be held responsible in that, for example, the illness may be believed to be a punishment for some past

crime, sin or transgression.

In return for these benefits, however, patients are expected to fulfil two obligations:

1. Patients must want to get well and should recognise that the sick role is only a temporary state, which they must want to leave behind. If they apparently do not want to get well then instead of the sick role being conferred by the medical practitioner, patients may be categorised as malingerers or hypochondriacs.
2. Patients must co-operate with technically competent help. The fact that it is only medical practitioners who can legitimately confer the sick role in our society ensures that the technically competent help tends to be confined to the official medical services. Patients who choose to defer to a lay person with claims to medical knowledge, in preference to a medical practitioner, are judged as not fulfilling one of the basic obligations of the sick role.

The patient's 'sick role', along with the professional role of the doctor in this relationship as suggested by Parsons, is summarised in Table 4.2.

Critics of Parsons' concept of the 'sick role' have taken him to task over its rigidity. Indeed we have already shown that help-seeking is problematic and we cannot always assume that the presence of symptoms leads to a demand for professional help. Kassebaum and Baumann (1965) have shown that the perception of illness and the subsequent routes to help-seeking varied between different ethnic groups, whilst in a study of New York residents, a great deal of variation in their expectations of the sick role was identified (Gordon, 1966). Further, although the notion of the sick role is undoubtedly very useful in explaining the illness behaviour of some people, particularly those with acute conditions, individuals with chronic conditions, and those with conditions having no immediately obvious cause – for example, myalgic encephalomyelitis (M.E.) – might not be seen to be eligible for assignation to the sick role. This is further complicated because the division between health and sickness may be blurred, the diagnosis and prognosis may be uncertain, and it may not be obvious what actions the patient could or should adopt to get well. This failure to encompass those with long term illness may explain

TABLE 4.2   *Analysis of the roles of patients and doctors
as suggested by Parsons*

Patient: sick role	Doctor: professional role
Obligations and Privileges	Expected to

1. Must want to get well as quickly as possible.

    1. Apply a high degree of skill and knowledge to the problems of illness.

2. Should seek professional medical advice and co-operate with doctor.

    2. Act for welfare of patient and community rather than for own self-interest, desire for money, advancement, etc.

3. Allowed (and may be expected) to shed some normal activities and responsibilities (e.g. employment, household tasks).

    3. Be objective and emotionally detached (i.e. should not judge patients' behaviour in terms of personal value system or become emotionally involved with them).

4. Regarded as being in need of care and unable to get better by his or her own decision and will.

    4. Be guided by rules of professional practice.

Rights:
1. Granted right to examine patients physically and to enquire into intimate areas of physical and personal life.

2. Granted considerable autonomy in professional practice.

3. Occupies position of authority in relation to patient.

Reproduced with permission from Patrick and Scambler (1986).

why doctors tend to be better disposed to those 'acute' specialities, such as general medicine and surgery, compared to dealing with chronic problems.

Other critics have argued that Parsons' sick role is biased in favour of medicine. That is, the definition of illness which authorises entry to this role is the definition of the medical profession, not that of the patient, and as such cannot adequately account for the patient's attitudes, beliefs and experiences, all of which contribute towards illness behaviour (Mechanic and Volkart, 1960). This particular criticism has focused attention on the process which leads the patient to consult with a doctor. Freidson (1961, 1970) argues that prior to consulting a doctor, patients who experience symptoms initially discuss them with friends, relatives or colleagues. It is this referral group, rather than medicine, which, Freidson argues, defines the individual's experience of symptoms as illness. Consequently, a distinction has been suggested between the 'sick role' (sickness initially being defined by friends, relatives and colleagues) and the 'patient role' (concerning the role of the patients as defined by doctors).

4.6 RELATIONSHIPS BETWEEN PATIENTS AND HEALTH CARE PROFESSIONALS

Pharmacists are being encouraged to communicate with patients, and patients are encouraged to seek advice from their pharmacist. So what form might the relationship between patients and pharmacists take? To our knowledge there have been no detailed sociological studies of the interactions between pharmacists and patients. The general practitioner-patient relationship, however, has been extensively studied in medical sociology and we shall consider this literature because it is likely to have implications for other health professions. We have already discussed Parsons' work on the 'sick role', which has defined the respective roles of patient and doctor. As conceived by Parsons, the interaction between health professionals and patients comprises what may be termed a consensual relationship. That is to say, that the relationship between the two is one of stable interaction, with both participants assuming shared expectations and values. According to Parsons such values are internalised through the process of socialisation.

Society is seen to function harmoniously; for example, the medical profession serves the functions of treating and legitimising illness, whilst patients acknowledge the authority of the medical profession to do so, i.e. the doctor-patient relationship is reciprocal in nature.

Another development of the consensus approach to professional-patient relationships was developed by Szasz and Hollender (1956). They identified three different forms that the relationship might take, although they still assumed an essentially reciprocal relationship.

As can be seen from Table 4.3, Szasz and Hollender describe three types of consultation:

First, the activity/passivity relationship, where the patient passively receives treatment, for example in the operating theatre. Second, the guidance/co-operation relationship, where the doctor tells the patient what to do in the case of acute illness, for example, the treatment of an infection. Third, the mutual participation relationship, where the doctor helps the patient to help him or herself, for example, modification of diet in the treatment of obesity.

We might suppose the mutual participation model would be the most appropriate for the community pharmacist because, as we have seen, patients have been encouraged to seek health care advice from pharmacists, so that they can practise self-care. The consensus approach to the doctor-patient relationship always assumes the health professional to be an authority and the patient content to be deferential. It has been argued, however, that we cannot assume reciprocity, nor can we assume a shared system

TABLE 4.3   *Szasz and Hollender's three models*
of patient-health professional relationship

Model	Physician's role	Patient's Role
Activity/passivity	Does something to the patient.	Recipient (unable to respond).
Guidance/co-operation	Tells patient what to do.	Co-operation (obeys).
Mutual participation	Helps patients to help themselves.	Participant in 'partnership'.

Reproduced with permission from Patrick and Scambler (1986).

of values and expectations. In contrast to the consensus approach, we must also consider conflict models. Freidson, for example, saw as inherent in the professional-patient relationship a 'clash of perspectives'. The professional and the patient have different values, ideas, priorities, interests, goals and knowledge. Indeed, as we have seen, lay people often have elaborate ideas about the causes of illness which, whilst they are inherently rational, may not necessarily match those of the medical profession. Consequently, Freidson has noted that 'the separate worlds of experience and reference of the lay person and of the professional worker are always in potential conflict with each other' (Freidson, 1975).

Bloor and Horobin (1975) see that conflict is implicit in the doctor-patient relationship. They point out that '. . .the sick person is first encouraged to participate in and then excluded from the therapeutic process.' Parsons' assumption of reciprocity is thus suspect. Patients are encouraged to assess their own symptoms accurately and yet to adopt a passive and deferential role once they enter the surgery. Indeed British doctors find the presentation by patients of 'trivial' conditions to be one of the most frustrating aspects of their work (Cartwright, 1967). This places the patient in what Bloor and Horobin refer to as a 'double blind situation'.

Doctors, because of their social status and prestige, are in a more powerful position in the consultation than the patient. They are able to control the events in the surgery and so there is very rarely open conflict between the two parties. Whilst doctors may appear to be in authority, the patients may not necessarily be wholly passive. Stimson and Webb (1975) in their book, *Going to See the Doctor*, have illustrated how patients may in fact practise subtle forms of negotiation with the doctor during the consultation.

4.7 CONSULTING A GENERAL PRACTITIONER

As we have illustrated in chapter three, a person is likely to consult a health professional when the perceived benefits outweigh the perceived costs. A visit to the general practitioner might include three potential benefits:

1. Treatment and therapy
2. Legitimation of sick role status
3. Advice and/or reassurance.

People often visit their general practitioner because they hope that he or she will be able to provide treatment which will alleviate their symptoms. The general practitioner may be able to make a diagnosis, suggest a prognosis, and offer treatment accordingly. Many cases, however, are not so clear cut and a degree of uncertainty enters into the consultation – this is often the case where the doctor, who is working within the medical model (Chapter 5), cannot find a pathological cause for a problem. A second reason for visiting a general practitioner may be to legitimate one's status as a patient. An obvious example of this is where employers may require a 'sick note' that confirms the employee's 'illness', or in the case of welfare benefits which are only granted on the basis of a doctor's decision. The doctor has, as we have seen in section 4.5, the social and legal authority to grant this status.

Finally, a visit to the doctor may arise out of uncertainty or anxiety about certain physical or mental states and patients may seek reassurances that their 'condition' is neither harmful nor abnormal. Because of the social prestige granted to doctors, some people may feel that the doctor can offer sound advice on aspects of their social lives, social relationships and so on. Some critics have argued that such growing dependency on doctors is a detrimental side-effect of their profession's monopoly (Illich, 1974; Zola, 1973).

4.8 CONSULTING A PHARMACIST

Whilst a patient having a particularly acute symptom, such as a growth or severe bleeding, will almost invariably consult a hospital or community-based medical practitioner, a patient with a mild symptom such as sunburn, an insect bite reaction, a hangover, slight graze or cut may be inclined to consult a pharmacist. These examples of acute and minor symptoms could be said to represent the extremes of a spectrum of symptoms. Between them there are a large number and range of symptoms with which both general practitioners and pharmacists may be capable of dealing. However, it would seem reasonable to speculate that symptoms which are perceived by the individual to be trivial are more likely to be presented to the pharmacist than symptoms perceived to be severe. The pharmacist can therefore offer appropriate treatment and advice for such minor symptoms. Beyond their conventional therapeutic role, pharmacists offer patients several other services.

Confirmation of health status

The concept of 'illness behaviour' has been offered to explain the changes in behaviour associated with becoming ill (see Chapter 3). Though the doctor plays a fundamental role in assisting the transition from 'person' to 'patient', the pharmacist often facilitates the change by giving credibility to the individual's symptoms as serious enough to warrant treatment, and possibly the attention of the doctor. Instructions on how to administer prescribed medicines consolidates this change in status from person to patient by reinforcing the message that being ill requires compliance with the instruction of health care professionals. The doctor may instruct a patient to take plenty of rest as part of the treatment regimen, while the pharmacist might instruct the patient on the consequences of non-compliance with the prescribed regimen. More often, however, people adopt different behaviour patterns which ease their transition from person to patient.

Availability and accessibility

The decision to consult a general practitioner involves a process of weighing up the costs and benefits to the patient. Costs such as loss of earnings, time and arranging an appointment may or may not outweigh any perceived benefits. Consultations in a pharmacy require no prior appointment, and pharmacies are available in most communities. The accessibility and ready availability of both the pharmacist and counter staff (often trained) provide unparalleled service for opportunistic health care advice and treatment. Patients do not have to register with a pharmacist, as they do with a general practitioner. Patients can therefore choose which pharmacist to consult, and may do so on the basis of gender, ethnicity and age. This may be a particular advantage when seeking advice, for example, about sexual problems, family planning, menstruation, laxatives and haemorrhoids.

Information source and supplier of unorthodox treatments

Pharmacists are a ready source of impartial information about unorthodox medical treatments such as homeopathy, vitamins, health foods, and herbalism.

Major source for dispensing prescriptions

The vast majority (95 per cent) of all prescriptions in Great Britain are dispensed from a pharmacy (the remainder being accounted for by dispensing doctors). Consequently patients (or their relatives or guardians) are most likely to visit a pharmacy in addition to having consulted the prescriber. This provides the opportunity for patients to seek clarification on their medication and discuss related or unrelated health matters.

Thus we have seen that the procedure for seeking professional health care is complex. The mediating effects of the lay referral system on an individual's decision whether or not to seek professional health care are an effective 'filter' to the uptake of health services. Parsons' concept of the 'sick role' highlights the complexity of the relationship between those who seek these services and those who provide them. A knowledge of this complexity is important in that it enables pharmacists to appreciate people's health-related experiences, and the factors which may bear on those who use health services.

Further Reading

Morgan, M. *et al.* (1985) *Sociological Approaches to Health and Medicine*, London, Routledge and Kegan Paul. Chapters Two and Three.
Fitzpatrick, R. *et al.* (1984) *The Experience of Illness*, London, Tavistock. Chapter Two.

References

Allen, G. (1985) *Family Life: Domestic Roles and Social Organisation*, Oxford, Basil Blackwell.
Apple, D. (1960) How Laymen Define Illness, *Human Behaviour*, 1: 219–225.

Becker, M. H. (1974) *The Health Belief Model and Personal Health Behaviour*, New Jersey, Charles B. Slack Inc.

Blaxter, M. (1983) The Causes of Disease: Women Talking, *Social Science and Medicine*, 17: 59–69.

Bloor, M. and Horobin, G. (1975) Conflict and Conflict Resolution in Doctor-Patient Interactions, in Cox C. and Mead M.E. (eds.) *A Sociology of Medical Practice*, London, Collier-Macmillan.

Blumhagen, D. (1980) Hyper-Tension: A Folk Illness with a Medical Name, *Culture, Medicine and Psychiatry*, 4: 197–227.

Calnan, M. (1984) The Health Belief Model and Participation Programmes for the Early Detection of Breast Cancer: A Comparative Analysis, *Social Science and Medicine*, 19: 823–830.

Cartwright, A. (1967) *Patients and their Doctors: A Study of General Practice*, London, Routledge and Kegan Paul.

Chrisman, N. J. (1977) The Health Seeking Process: An Approach to the Natural History of Illness, *Culture, Medicine and Society*, 1: 351–377.

Fitzpatrick, R., Hinton, J., Newman, S., Scambler, G. and Thompson, J. (1984) *The Experience of Illness*, London, Tavistock.

Freidson, E. (1975) Dilemmas in the Doctor Patient Relationship, in Cox, C. and Mead, A. (eds.) *A Sociology of Medical Practice*, London, Collier-Macmillan.

Freidson, E. (1961) *Patients' Views of Medical Practice*, New York, Russell Sage Foundation.

Freidson, E. (1970) *Profession of Medicine, a Study of the Sociology of Applied Knowledge*, New York, Harper & Row.

Gordon, G. (1966) *Role Theory and Illness: a Sociological Perspective*, New Haven, College and University Press.

Illich, I. (1974) *Medical Nemesis*, London, Calder Boyars.

Kassebaum, G. G. and Baumann, B. O. (1965) Dimensions of the Sick Role in Chronic Illness, *Journal of Health and Human Behaviour*, 6: 16–27.

McKinlay, J. B. (1973) Social Networks, Lay Consultations, and Help-Seeking Behaviour, *Social Forces*, 51: 255–292.

Mechanic, D. and Volkart, E. (1960) Illness Behaviour and Medical Diagnosis, *Journal of Health and Human Behaviour*, 1: 86–94.

Parsons, T. (1951) *The Social System*, London, Free Press.

Patrick, D. and Scambler, G. (eds.) (1986) *Sociology as Applied to Medicine*, London, Bailliere Tindall.

Rosenstock, I. (1966) Why People Use Health Services, *Milbank Memorial Fund Quarterly*, 44: 94–127.

Stacey, M. (1988) *The Sociology of Health and Healing*, London, Unwin Hyman.

Stimson, G. V. and Webb, B. (1975) *Going to See the Doctor*, London, Routledge and Kegan Paul.

Szasz, T. S. and Hollender, M. H. (1956) A Contribution to the

Philosophy of Medicine: the Basic Models of the Doctor-Patient Relationship, *Archives of International Medicine*, 97: 585–592.

Taylor, J. (1979) Hidden Labour in the National Health Service, in: Atkinson, P., Dingwall, R., and Murcott, A. (eds.) *Prospects for National Health*, London, Croom Helm.

Warwick, I., Aggleton, P., and Homans, H. (1988) Constructing Common Sense – Young People's Beliefs About AIDS, *Sociology of Health and Illness*, 10: 213–233.

Williams, G. H. and Wood, P. H. (1986) Common Sense Beliefs about Illness: A Mediating Role for the Doctor, *Lancet* ii, 8522: 1435.

Zola, I. K. (1973) Pathways to the Doctor: From Person to Patient, *Social Science and Medicine*, 7: 677–689.

5 Social Factors and Health

In this chapter we shall consider how disease may from one perspective be considered as having specific biological causes, whilst from another perspective it may be seen as having social, economic and environmental causes. First we will need to consider how we can best measure health within a given population or subsection of that population.

5.1 MEASURING HEALTH

Measures of health status are notoriously complex. Existing data relating to mortality (deaths) and morbidity (disease) have yielded valuable evidence of the inequitable distribution of health chances in the community. It should be appreciated, however, that such measures are inherently problematic. It is important that we clarify what is meant by these epidemiological indicators.

Mortality rates

Mortality or death rates are usually presented as the number of deaths per 1000 living members of a population per year. The crude death rate will be affected by the demographic composition of the population. Therefore age-specific death rates can be calculated thus:

$$\frac{\text{number of deaths of a given age}}{\text{number in population at that age}} \times 1000$$

These may also be calculated separately for men and women and for different occupational categories. These are then 'standardised' death or mortality rates. The standardised mortality rate is a method of comparing death rates between different sections of the population while holding other variables constant, e.g. comparing one geographical area with another, whilst holding age, sex and occupation constant.

Mortality rates – which are regarded as particularly important indicators of social welfare, circumstances and health status –, are the neonatal, perinatal and infant mortality rates. These measures are calculated in the following ways (Macfarlane and Mugford, 1984):

Neonatal mortality rate:

$$\frac{\text{Deaths at 0–27 days after live birth} \times 1000}{\text{Live births}}$$

Perinatal mortality rate:

$$\frac{(\text{Stillbirths} + \text{deaths at 0–6 days after live birth}) \times 1000}{\text{Live births} + \text{stillbirths}}$$

Infant mortality rate:

$$\frac{\text{Deaths under the age of one year after live birth} \times 1000}{\text{Live births}}$$

Morbidity incidence, prevalence and rates

Morbidity refers to sickness or disease. The incidence of a disease is the number of times it occurs, i.e. the number of cases contracted or resulting in death, in a given social group within a given period of time, e.g. how many new cases are reported in a year. The prevalence of a disease is the total number of cases, i.e. the number of people suffering from the disease in a given time. The distribution of disease in different populations may be adjusted to take into account the size of the population. This process results in ratios where the number of cases of the disease (the prevalence or incidence) is divided by the number of people in the population. Because these ratios often result in very small numbers the ratio is multiplied by 1000. This has the effect of producing a ratio which indicates how many cases of disease exist per 1000.

The morbidity rate then, is calculated thus:

$$\frac{\text{Number of people with disease in the population}}{\text{Number of people in the population}} \times 1000$$

Rates may be further calculated for specific sub-groups, e.g. to produce age-specific, sex-specific or occupation-specific morbidity rates. MacIntyre (1988) has highlighted some problems associated with using mortality and morbidity rates as indicators of health. She points out that mortality rates are increasingly unreliable since:

1. Reductions of mortality rates to low levels in industrialised countries make comparisons unreliable because of the small numbers involved.
2. With the overall increase in life expectancy and a considerably smaller proportion of deaths occurring before the age of 65 years than in the past, data on the economically active is based on smaller proportions of the total population.
3. Mortality rates clearly cannot measure improvement, stability or deterioration in health.
4. Mortality rates are based on a binary division of dead or alive and therefore they are not sensitive to degrees of healthiness of those still alive.
5. With changes in the nature of disease, i.e. with an increase in chronic and degenerative diseases and the overall decrease in infectious diseases, mortality rates are less useful because, although they are falling, morbidity may at the same time be increasing.
6. Morbidity rates and mortality rates have sometimes been found to be at odds for certain social groups, for example, women live longer than men yet have higher rates of morbidity.

MacIntyre has also set out the shortcomings of morbidity measures:

1. Morbidity measures which are based on the uptake of health services, for example, how many people visit their general practitioner, are often used as indicators of morbidity. However such measures may tell us more about the nature and availability of service provision than about morbidity.
2. Self-reported data of health are based on the individual's concepts and perceptions of symptoms and illness. Clearly interpretations of these may vary between groups which the researcher might be seeking to compare.

3. There are known variations in diagnostic conventions between countries and these also change over time, making
   comparisons between time and place potentially unreliable.

These difficulties encountered in measuring health, like the use
of occupation as an indicator of social class, do not imply that the
existing data has no value. Rather, in drawing attention to these
difficulties, we are seeking to emphasise the nature of the subject
matter we hope to understand. We must be constantly vigilant in
our methods of collecting and interpreting data because the social
world by its very nature cannot be explained or understood by
definite concepts or static measures.

5.2 PERSPECTIVES ON HEALTH

During the last few decades there has been a transformation in
the way certain elements of medicine and medical practice are
comprehended. The academic disciplines of medical sociology and
epidemiology, along with social movements such as consumer
groups and women's movements (Ehrenreich, 1978), have begun
to challenge orthodox medical ideas; in particular, they have challenged bio-medical explanations of the causes of disease.

In the nineteenth and early twentieth centuries disease was
believed to be the direct consequence of specific causal agents such
as bacteria or viruses. This has been referred to as the 'doctrine of
specific aetiology' (Dubos, 1959). Today, however, disease is recognised as being the product of both biological and social factors.
In order to explain the occurrence of disease it is now necessary to
appreciate the socio-environmental context in which disease arises
and to recognise that, in addition to having a biological cause,
disease may also be the result of social and psychological factors.
For example, the role that stress and diet play in determining
health status has been increasingly recognised in conditions such
as coronary disease.

In broadening the scope beyond purely biological explanations
of disease to include social and psychological factors, some of the
earlier claims of medicine have become subject to scrutiny. In the
early 1970s an influential body of work emerged which, although
originating from within the medical profession, was critical of
the assumption that medical intervention alone could ameliorate

disease. One such critic, McKeown (1979), by way of a complex historical demographic study illustrated that the rapid decline in the population's death rate which occurred in the eighteenth and nineteenth centuries was due to a reduction in communicable diseases. This decline, he argued, had little to do with medical interventions such as immunisation programmes, but was due initially to increases in food supplies, and subsequently to better hygiene and sanitation, and to an increased acceptance of methods of birth control. As McKeown argues,

If we group together the advances in nutrition and hygiene as environmental measures, the influences responsible for the decline of mortality and associated improvement in health were environmental, behavioural and therapeutic. They became effective from the eighteenth, nineteenth and twentieth centuries respectively and their order in time was also that of their effectiveness.

Considering tuberculosis as a specific example, McKeown demonstrated that a large part of the decline in the death rate from tuberculosis in England and Wales occurred before the introduction of streptomycin in 1947.

As we can see from Figure 5.1, treatment with streptomycin reduced the number of deaths between 1948–1971 by 51 per cent but when considered over the period from 1848–1971 the reduction in the number of deaths was only 3.2 per cent. The challenge to the effectiveness, appropriateness and superiority of Western medicine has been made not only by certain epidemiologists, such as McKeown, but also by other groups. The women's movement, for example, has effectively demonstrated that the medical profession has only a partial understanding of health and illness and that medicine's faith in technology has at times blinded the profession when it comes to the type of care it offers. For instance, if we consider childbirth: this essentially natural process has come to be associated with a never ending array of clinical tests, checks, screening procedures and so on. Some more radical commentators on medicine and medical practice such as Illich (1975) have argued that medical intervention, through its procedures, can be iatrogenic, i.e. result in more harm than good.

Illich sees the impact of medicine as harmful on three levels, he refers to these as 'clinical', 'social' and 'cultural' iatrogenesis.

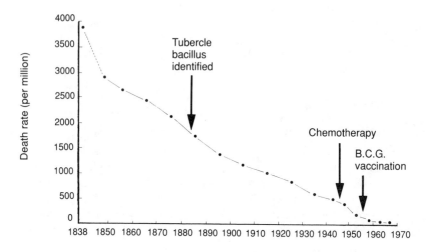

FIGURE 5.1   Respiratory tuberculosis: annual death rates
for England and Wales 1838–1970
Reproduced with permission from McKeown (1979).

Clinical iatrogenesis refers to all those conditions for which 'remedies, physicians, or hospitals are the pathogens': he supports
his argument with data that shows how drugs administered to
patients have deleterious sides effects on a scale that must be
unacceptable; and how surgical intervention often has unintended
and negative results. On the second level, medicine reinforces
'social over-medicalisation' in that more and more aspects of our
lives come under the remit of medicine and, consequently many
social problems are neutralised and become removed from the
political arena. Furthermore, Illich suggests that the presence of
a medical profession which over the past two centuries has established a monopoly over medical knowledge and practice has generated a 'culture of dependence'. The lay public, Illich argues, has
become reliant on medicine to the point that they no longer feel
capable of caring for themselves. This dependence on so-called
'experts' constitutes cultural iatrogenesis.

One consequence of these criticisms of the role of medicine in
health care has been the development of two approaches to health
and disease. These are the 'medical model' which comprises the
'germ theory' of disease, and the 'socio-environmental model',

which associates disease with nutrition, hygiene, environmental and behavioural factors.

5.3 THE MEDICAL MODEL OF HEALTH AND DISEASE

The 'germ theory' of disease which emerged in the nineteenth century came to be the main form of explanation in scientific medicine. Thus it constituted the dominant intellectual framework or 'paradigm' within which medicine worked and this framework has been loosely termed the 'medical model'. This model represents a set of basic assumptions held by medical scientists about the nature and causes of health and disease. These assumptions included:

1. All disease can be traced to a specific aetiology such as virus, parasite, or bacterium.
2. The patient's body can be treated like a machine in that it is passive during treatment, and can be made better through medical 'engineering'.
3. The elimination of disease and the return to health depend on medical technology and/or chemical intervention.

5.4 THE SOCIO-ENVIRONMENTAL MODEL OF HEALTH AND DISEASE

The 'socio-environmental' model of health and disease involves a change of emphasis from that of the 'medical model'. Whilst the medical model emphasises the impact of medicine in the elimination of disease, the 'socio-environmental' model emphasises the maintenance and production of good health. This takes place through environmental and behavioural changes. In other words, where and how people live their lives are regarded as being just as significant as biological factors in determining their health status. A corollary to this is that people are no longer seen as passive victims of disease, but can themselves participate in the production of good health. Prevention is also seen to be preferable to intervention (see Chapter 8).

Whilst in the 'medical model', health was defined by an absence of disease, a rather negative and a purely functional concept in that it implies being physically and mentally able, the 'socio-environmental' model has yielded a broader definition. The World Health Organisation, for example, has defined health as 'a state of complete physical, mental and social well being and not merely the absence of disease or infirmity.'

An important consequence of this development has been that health cannot and should not be separated from the social environment in which a person lives. Just as the decline of infectious disease during the nineteenth century was the result of improved nutrition, hygiene and birth control, the common 'killers' of the twentieth century – heart disease/circulatory disorders, cancer (for adults), and accidents (for children) – are all associated with factors such as occupation, stress, diet, smoking, pollution and environment.

Further Reading

Hart, N. (1985) *The Sociology of Health and Medicine*, Ormskirk, Causeway Press. Chapters One and Two.

Illich, I. (1974) *Medical Nemesis*, London, Calder Boyars.

McKeown, T. (1979) *The Role of Medicine: Dream, Mirage or Nemesis*, Oxford, Blackwell.

References

Dubos, R. (1959) *Mirage of Health*, New York, Harper & Row.

Ehrenreich, J. (ed.) (1978) *The Cultural Crisis of Modern Medicine*, London, Monthly Review Press.

Illich, I. (1975) *Limits to Medicine*, London, Marion Boyars.

Macfarlane, A. and Mugford, M. (1984) *Birth Counts: Statistics of Pregnancy and Childbirth*, London, HMSO.

MacIntyre, S. (1988) A Review of the Social Patterning and Significance of Measures of Height, Weight, Blood Pressure, and Respiratory Function, *Social Science and Medicine*, 27: 327–337.

McKeown, T. (1979) *The Role of Medicine: Dream, Mirage or Nemesis*, Oxford, Blackwell.

6 Social Inequalities and Health

This chapter will illustrate that health and disease are not simply biologically determined phenomena and that the chances of
becoming ill are frequently related to a person's social circumstances. That is to say, illness and disease are not simply associated
with physiological changes but are also influenced by where we
live, and how we live, work, and eat, and also by our relationships
with other people. We shall examine the evidence which shows
that disease has a social, as well as a biological basis – in fact, that
disease is socially patterned. By this we mean that certain groups
of people in society are more likely to suffer from certain ailments
than others. Generally those people most susceptible to such ailments are those who have the fewest material resources, and
whose access to decent housing, adequate transport and employment opportunities is most restricted.

Western society is manifestly unequal; people are placed hier-
archically along dimensions of inequality such as age, income,
occupation, gender and ethnicity, and some may subsequently
suffer because of their position in society. The level at which
members of a given social strata find themselves can influence
their life chances, or their opportunities to achieve rewards in
society, be they satisfactory careers, housing, income or health. We
shall explore these dimensions of inequality in relation to health.

6.1 GENDER AND HEALTH

One important dimension of inequality is the result of social
relations between men and women, that is, gender relations.
Gender refers to the socially constructed differentiation between
men and women, while sex refers to the biological distinction
between males and females. As we shall see later in this chapter,
people in higher occupational categories have social and economic
advantages, similarly men have social and economic advantages

TABLE 6.1   *Longstanding illness by social class and sex in Great Britain*
Morbidity rates per 1000.

Social Class	Male	Female
I	111	111
II	131	136
III Non manual	157	169
III Manual	175	170
IV	196	234
V	233	282
All Persons	168	185

Adapted from Meredith Davies (1983).

over women. There is inequality between men and women in the family; women do more housework than men, and this is the case even when women are in full-time employment (Gershuny, 1983). Similarly, domestic resources such as the family car and money are not equally shared between men and women in the same household (Graham, 1984). Moreover, women frequently earn less than men, and they are more likely to work part-time. Gender, then, as a form of stratification, is of particular relevance to health and health care. There are higher rates of morbidity among women than among men. As can be seen in Table 6.1, women as a group not only tend to suffer higher rates of morbidity than men, but those in social classes IV and V have higher rates of morbidity, compared with women within other social classes. The relationship between social class and health is discussed as a separate issue in section 6.6.

However, although women have higher rates of morbidity than men, they do live longer. As can be seen in Table 6.2, during the twentieth century the life expectancy of both males and females has steadily increased. Consistently women could expect to outlive men. Currently, on average, women live six years longer than men. The discrepancy between the mortality and morbidity rates for males and females has been explored by sociologists. Waldron (1983) in her paper, 'Sex Differences in Illness Incidence', discusses some of the possible reasons for this difference. The discrepancy may be a function of the research methods employed, for example, in studies where people report their own incidence of illness, men may be more likely to feel that illness is a sign of weakness and hence under-report the incidence of illness. Furthermore, women

TABLE 6.2   *Expectation of life at birth by sex, from 1900–79,*
in England and Wales

Year	Expectation of life (years)	
	Male	Female
1900–02	48.5	52.4
1910–12	51.5	55.4
1920–22	55.6	59.6
1930–32	58.7	62.9
1950–52	66.4	71.5
1960–62	68.1	74.0
1970–72	69.0	75.3
1977–79	70.2	76.4

Adapted from Meredith Davies (1983).

are found to be more predisposed to take responsibility for their health than men, explaining womens' higher rates of morbidity derived from working days lost or visits to the general practitioner. It has also been argued that men are more inclined to take risks with their health, whilst women are more likely to adopt preventive behaviours.

6.2   ETHNICITY AND HEALTH

Another dimension of inequality in western societies is that between the white population and ethnic minorities. Donovan (1984) provides a definition which give us a useful starting point for discussion:

> 'minority', 'ethnic' or 'ethnic minority' group is used to describe any group of people who share a cultural heritage, are not part of the majority, and may experience varying degrees of discrimination . . .)

Inequality between ethnic groups results from discrimination predominantly on the basis of skin colour. Race or ethnicity need to be considered because they are strongly related to an individual's life chances and opportunities (Rathwell and Phillips, 1986) and these are major determinants of health.

As we have discussed, Western society is unequal; this inequality manifests itself in lessened life and health chances on the basis of social class, gender and occupation. When these factors are combined with ethnic differences, the result is often a degree of prejudice and discrimination that may also be important influences on health status and the experience of health care.

Data on ethnicity and health is limited. Moreover, research in this field has tended to focus on specific illnesses such as rickets, thalassaemia, tuberculosis, hypertension, sickle cell anaemia and mental health (Table 6.3).

Whilst not wanting to underplay the importance and significance of these diseases for those who suffer from them, it is important to remember that people of ethnic minorities in the main suffer from the same illnesses as the rest of the population. As Donovan (1984) has pointed out, the study of ethnicity and health has revolved '. . . principally around a few major illnesses and diseases that have captured the attention of medical and other health professionals, but which affect a relatively small number of people. Although these illnesses are important and need treatment, they do not represent the everyday health problems that most black people have to contend with.' The everyday health problems that black people have to contend with, she indicates, are the same as

TABLE 6.3   *Comparison of mortality rates:*
specific mortality by racial group (England and Wales)

Cause of Mortality	Comparison with rates in England and Wales
Tuberculosis	Highest among individuals originating from Indian subcontinent, Africa, Caribbean, Scotland and Ireland.
Liver Cancer	High among individuals originating from Indian subcontinent, Caribbean and Africa.
Hypertension and Stroke	Strikingly high among individuals originating from Caribbean and Africa.
Maternal Mortality	High amongst individuals originating from Caribbean and Africa.

Adapted from Marmot *et al.* (1984).

those of white people.

One such everyday health problem concerns the use of health services. In a study of the experiences of patients suffering from sickle cell anaemia, presenting themselves at the Accident and Emergency Department of an East London Hospital, Black and Laws (1986) found that the patients or the patients' parents met with ignorance on the part of medical staff and received little sympathy. The authors described cases of mothers being accused of battering their children who were in pain from sickle cell anaemia. This, they claimed, 'shows alarming readiness to mistrust and blame the mother rather than investigate the physical problems'. They also pointed to the need for health professionals to have an understanding of the disease, otherwise false conclusions about the presenting symptoms are easily drawn. False diagnosis can also be made from symptoms when the assessor too readily makes assumptions about what they consider to be 'normal'. For example, over-representation of black people purporting to be sufferers of mental illness has been found to reflect the assumptions held by psychiatrists, who 'label' people as 'mentally ill' because they have failed to fully appreciate the reasons for the patient's thoughts and behaviour (Littlewood and Cross, 1980).

6.3 THE CONCEPT OF SOCIAL CLASS

If we consider the distribution of diseases, it is apparent that some diseases are more prevalent among some members of the community than others. Therefore the distribution of disease cannot be considered a purely random event to which every individual is equally susceptible. Moreover an individual's prospect of longevity, and the quality of their health in general, owes less to chance and more to a number of predetermined factors. This discrepancy in the distribution of health and illness is particularly noticeable among the socially disadvantaged.

One of the most easily identifiable and most frequently talked about inequalities existing within British society is that of social class. Social class is regarded by some sociologists as the most fundamental system of social stratification within capitalist societies. The origins of class analysis can be traced back to the work of Karl Marx and the German sociologist Max Weber. Both sought

to describe and explain the new class structure which emerged
with the growth of industrial capitalism in early nineteenth century
Europe. Although their explanations of the origins and consequences of social class differed, they both believed class to be
associated with economic circumstances. The origins, nature and
implications of social class in the capitalist world are the subject
of much debate within sociology. This need not unduly concern
us here, but it is important to remember that social class, like
all sociological concepts, is not static and unchanging, but rather
refers to a fluid or dynamic phenomenon. The eminent historian,
E. P. Thompson illustrates this point with clarity in his work, *The
Making of the English Working Class* (1977):

> Sociologists who have stopped the time machine and, with a
> good deal of conceptual huffing and puffing, have gone down
> to the engine-room to look, tell us that no where at all have
> they been able to locate and classify a class. They can only
> find a multitude of people with different occupations, incomes,
> status-hierarchies, and the rest. Of course they are right, since
> class is not this or that part of the machine, but the way the
> machine works once it is set in motion – not this and that inter-
> est, but the friction of interests – the movement itself, the heat,
> the thundering noise. Class is a social and cultural formation
> (often finding institutional expression) which cannot be defined
> abstractly, or in isolation, but only in terms of relationships with
> other classes: and, ultimately, the definition can only be made
> in the medium of time – that is, action and reaction, change and
> conflict. When we speak of a class we are thinking of a very
> loosely defined body of people who share the same congeries of
> interests, social experiences, traditions and value-systems, who
> have a disposition to behave as a class, to define themselves
> in their actions and in their consciousness in relation to other
> groups of people in class ways. But class itself is not a thing, it
> is a happening.

6.4   SOCIAL CLASS CLASSIFICATION

While gender and ethnicity are significant forms of stratification,
social class has been used more extensively as an indicator of
material circumstances. When we read a government document or

TABLE 6.4   *The Registrar General's social class classification*

	Social Class	Examples of Occupation
I	Professional	Doctor, lawyer, pharmacist
II	Intermediate	School teacher, manager, nurse
IIINM	Skilled non–manual	Secretary, shop assistant
IIIM	Skilled manual	Carpenter, electrician, cook
IV	Partly skilled	Postman, bus conductor, machinist
V	Unskilled	Cleaner, labourer, dock worker

hear reports of research findings which are related to social class, these are most likely to be based on one of two types of classification which divide the population into a hierarchy of categories based on occupation. These are the Registrar General's social class classification and the Socio-Economic Group's Classification which is used in the General Household Survey. These two classifications are similar, and for illustration the Registrar General's classification is reproduced in Table 6.4.

6.5   LIMITATIONS OF SOCIAL CLASSIFICATION SYSTEMS

Any classification system based simply on occupation has a number of shortcomings. To begin with, these systems are based on a hierarchy of occupations which fail to fully take into account the continually changing nature of work patterns. For example, professional and managerial occupations have expanded rapidly, especially in the service or tertiary industries such as the financial, education and health sectors. There has also been a change in the nature of clerical work over the latter half of this century. This change has not merely involved the introduction of technology into offices but has also resulted in an increased number of women recruited into this skilled, non-manual sector.

The classifications in terms of occupation may well be misleading, as women in non-manual occupations, which are classified as higher than manual work, may well receive lower pay than male manual workers, or be employed on a part-time basis. Moreover, there has been a substantial decline in the number of people in manual work. Manufacturing industries such as mining, shipbuilding and textiles have declined in recent years, whilst service industries have expanded.

Clearly occupational categories fail to take into account those people who are not working or, more accurately, those who are not economically active, such as the unemployed, retired, some people with disabilities, and women who work at home. Domestic work, which makes a significant contribution to the economy, has been neglected in the development of classifications of social class. Further, when classifying families only the occupation of the head of the household is taken into account. This may not accurately reflect the household in which other members may add significantly to the overall income. When classifying families on the basis of the occupation of the head of the household there is also an assumption that the income and the associated resources are distributed equitably within the family. In practice, this has been shown not to be the case – for example a resource such as the 'family car' frequently used by the husband was rarely available to the wife on a daily basis (Graham, 1984).

Despite these shortcomings, and in the absence of more sensitive measures, occupational categories provide an appropriate means of collating data which can be related to people's socio-economic circumstances. Consequently, we shall consider how these socio-economic indicators can be related to health status.

6.6 SOCIAL CLASS AND HEALTH: THE EVIDENCE

The significance of social class in relation to health is that it is an indicator of material resources, i.e. income, wealth, material possessions and lifestyle. Indeed the Report of the Working Group on Inequalities in Health, which was submitted to the Secretary of State for Health in 1980, defined social class as: '. . . segments of the population sharing broadly similar styles of living and (for some sociologists) some shared perception of their collective condition' (Townsend and Davidson, 1982). This report, widely referred to as the Black Report (after its chairman Sir Douglas Black), provided extensive evidence of inequalities in health status and of the use, availability and provision of health services between different social groups. The findings and recommendations of the Black Report resulted in a great deal of controversy at the time. In

TABLE 6.5   *Stillbirth and mortality rates in the first year of life
for legitimate births by social class, 1979*

Social Group	Stillbirth*	Infant Mortality **
I	5.2	9.8
II	6.3	9.7
IIINM	6.8	9.8
IIIM	8.1	11.4
IV	9.3	14.3
V	9.6	18.7

* per thousand live and stillbirths.
** per thousand live births.
Adapted from OPCS (1982).

his response to the Report, the Health Secretary, Patrick Jenkin, noted that, 'It will come as a disappointment to many that over long periods since the inception of the NHS there is generally little sign of health inequalities in Britain actually diminishing and, in some cases they may be increasing.' Nevertheless, he felt that the proposals, which he claimed would cost upwards of two billion a year, were 'unrealistic' and he therefore would make no commitment to a change in existing health policy.

The Health Divide: Inequalities in the 1980s, published in 1987, examined how the picture had changed since the Black Report, and considered what progress, if any, had been made towards implementing the recommendations of the 1980 Working Group. It emerged that for most areas of health the social class inequalities remained. A striking example of the extent to which social class correlates with inequalities in health status is apparent from the statistics on rates of still-birth and infant mortality. Table 6.5 shows that women who were categorised as belonging to social groups one and two were least likely to have a still-born child, and had children with the lowest rates of infant mortality. Women categorised as belonging to social group five had a much higher rate of still-births, and a rate of infant mortality almost twice that of social group one. Thus it is apparent that the rates of both still-births and infant mortality are related to a person's social grouping.

There are however, some examples which indicate that this situation is not inevitable or insurmountable if the political will can be found to address the social causes of ill health. Whitehead, the author of *The Health Divide* (1987) found that:

The studies [in Health Divide] confirm the original conclusions of the [Black] report; that inequalities in health have widened since the 1950s. The exception to the widening trend is in relation to babies aged one month to one year. There was a dramatic decline in their health rates during the 1970s in all classes, but especially in class V, and thus the mortality gap narrowed considerably. Although there has been very little further improvement since 1980 for manual or non-manual classes the evidence does illustrate that the class differential is not inevitable. It can be reduced.

Infant mortality rates vary internationally as well as between subgroups within societies. Table 6.6 shows infant mortality rates for countries in the European Community. The rates for 1985 in all countries were considerably lower than in 1961. Those countries with the highest rates in 1961 (e.g. Portugal) have experienced the steepest reduction in those rates. Indeed, the fact that there are variations illustrates that infant mortality rates can be changed. What is important to remember is the reasons for the differences, which, as we have seen, are essentially due to socio-environmental factors such as nutrition, hygiene, and the health status of the mother.

TABLE 6.6   *Comparison of infant mortality rates for member countries of the European Community*

	1961	1971	1981	1985
United Kingdom	22.1	17.9	11.2	9.4
Belgium	28.1	20.4	11.5	9.4
Denmark	21.8	13.5	7.9	7.9
France	25.7	17.2	9.7	8.3
Germany (Fed. Rep.)	32.0	23.1	11.6	9.0
Greece	39.8	26.9	16.3	14.1
Irish Republic	30.5	18.0	10.3	8.9
Italy	40.7	28.5	14.1	10.3
Luxembourg	26.2	22.5	13.8	9.0
Netherlands	17.0	12.1	8.3	8.0
Portugal	88.8	51.9	21.8	17.8
Spain	46.2	25.7	10.3	—

Reproduced with permission from *Social Trends* (1988).

The poorest occupational groups also have the highest rates of death among people of working age and those who have retired. Men classified in group five are more than twice as likely to die between the ages of 16 and 64 years as men in group one. Similarly, married women classified in group five are nearly twice as likely to die between the ages of 20 and 59 years as married women in social class one (OPCS, 1986).

An association between occupation or social group and health chances has been explored further by Marmott and Theorell (1988). They have reviewed the evidence that psycho-social work conditions influence the risk factors associated with coronary heart disease. Those workers who have least skill and least discretion or authority over decisions, or who lack social support at work, were found to be most likely to experience stress and adopt unhealthy behaviour such as smoking. Hence, while the relationship between heart disease and stress and smoking has been established, this may not constitute an adequate explanation of a person's ill-health because there are often other factors associated with their social circumstances which should be taken into account.

Linked with inequalities in health between social groupings, there also exists marked differences in life expectancy according to geographical location. In a study of inequalities in health within the Northern Regional Health Authority, Townsend *et al.* (1986) reported significant differences in death rates for men and women between various geographical regions within Great Britain (Table 6.7). Moreover, within these regions there may also be marked differences in life expectancy. For example, a study in Sheffield found that there was a difference in life expectancy of almost eight years between the most affluent and the most deprived areas within the city (Thunhurst, 1985). This may be the outcome of factors such as people's occupations, their housing conditions and their exposure to environmental hazards such as road traffic, pollution and a lack of safe-play areas for children.

6.7   UNEMPLOYMENT AND HEALTH

Whilst certain occupations can result in detrimental effects on an individual's health, so too can being out of work. Fagin in his report, *The Forsaken Families: the Effects of Unemployment on*

TABLE 6.7   *Mortality rates of men and women*
in different regions of Britain, 1979–80, and 1982–83

Region	Direct age-standardised death rate (per 1000)		
	Men	Single Women	Married Women
	20–64	20–59	20–59
Central Clydeside	7.86	1.78	3.23
Strathclyde	7.14	1.66	3.06
North	6.43	1.56	2.50
North West	6.37	1.69	2.52
Remainder of Scotland	6.13	1.47	2.58
Wales	5.86	1.43	2.34
Yorks and Humberside	5.83	1.48	2.32
West Midlands	5.72	1.54	2.26
East Midlands	5.28	1.40	2.14
South East	4.88	1.29	1.97
South West	4.82	1.32	1.93
East Anglia	4.37	1.14	1.79
Scotland	6.92	1.62	2.89
England and Wales	5.43	1.41	2.89
Britain	5.57	1.43	2.23

Reproduced with permission from Townsend *et al.* (1986).

Family Life (1984), documented the extent to which financial worries resulting from unemployment had an impact on family tension. This tension was manifested in high rates of depression, asthma or headaches in all the family members. Similarly, a longitudinal study of twenty-six shipyard workers and their families (Joelson and Wahlquist, 1987) found that men who had been made redundant experienced depressive reactions, despite good financial compensation. A central theme of their findings was that when people lost their jobs they also felt they had lost their identity. Their previously structured lives had been disrupted, so that for example: 'work . . . regulates strain and rest and the time spent with one's family and away from it'. Work was also seen as evidence of the men's competence and knowledge. Whilst at work the men had clearly defined relations with other workers and with their work mates. On being made redundant most of the single men lost the majority of their social contacts.

Further evidence that people who are unemployed tend to have poorer health than those who are in employment has been provided by Maclure and Stewart, who found that 28 per cent of unemployed men reported longstanding illness, compared with 25 per cent of working men. Children of the unemployed were also found to be more prone to poor health. Data from the 1981 census was used to show that children living in deprived districts of Glasgow were more likely to be admitted to hospital than children in non-deprived districts (Maclure and Stewart, 1984).

We have provided only a brief introduction to an extensive literature on the relationship between social class and health. However from the studies in this area it is clearly evident that:

1. Inequalities in health apply at every stage of life, from birth throughout adult life to old age.
2. All the major killer diseases affect the poor more than the affluent.
3. Chronic sickness is more prevalent in the less favoured occupations.
4. The unemployed and their families have been found to experience poor mental and physical health.

6.8   SOCIAL CLASS AND HEALTH: THE EXPLANATIONS

As we have illustrated, there is extensive data suggesting the existence of a correlation between social class and health status. However evidence of a statistical correlation does not of itself provide us with an adequate explanation for the inequalities. The data only provides the starting point. Presented with such evidence we need to try and make sense of it and search for appropriate explanations. In other words we have seen that there is a relationship between two variables, social class and health; however, this relationship requires further explanation because we cannot be sure which is the causal variable simply by presenting the data. Methodologically, then, we need to identify which is the independent and which is the dependent variable. That is to say, does social class determine health, or health determine social class?

Some sociologists have argued that the reason for the inequalities in health is that people who experience poor health tend to move down the occupational scale. These sociologists regard a person's social class position as being dependent on their health (Goldberg and Morrison, 1963; Illsley, 1986). Wadsworth (1986) for example, using data from the National Survey of Health and Development Cohort Study, showed how a series of illnesses in childhood could affect social mobility. Boys who were seriously ill were more likely than others to experience a fall in occupational class by the time they were twenty-six years old, although others have argued that overall this effect is of a very minor nature (Blane, 1985). Conversely, it has been argued that health is dependent on an individual's socio-economic circumstances, i.e. their occupation, financial resources and standard of living. One variant of this perspective maintains that people from lower socio-economic groups may be less inclined to protect their future health and tend from an early age to adopt lifestyles that are potentially harmful. Another orientation of the view that health is the outcome of social class is that poor health may be attributed less to the individual and more to the individual's physical and social environment.

Both the Black Report and *The Health Divide* assessed the validity of the explanations which have formed the main strands of the debate concerning social class and health in recent decades. They have identified four explanations for the link between the two.

The artifact explanation

The artifact explanation proposes that health inequalities are artificial rather than real. They are merely a function of inadequate tools of measurement. That is to say the 'tools' or indicators used to establish a link between social class and health are not sufficiently sensitive for what they were intended to measure. The quality and reproducibility of the data, however, would seem to refute this argument.

The social selection explanation

The social selection explanation presents the case that we have outlined above, namely that health determines social class. The finding that health inequalities are related to social status is a consequence of the notion that those with good health tend to improve their social position, while those in poor health 'drift' downwards.

The cultural/behavioural explanation

Cultural/behavioural arguments claim that certain patterns of behaviour, for instance smoking, lack of exercise and excessive consumption of alcohol, are more prevalent amongst certain groups in society than others. This explanation assumes that the individual is able to overcome societal and environmental pressures to take up or continue these patterns of behaviour if they so desire.

The materialist or structuralist explanation

The materialist or structuralist postulate emphasises the circumstances in which people live. From this point of view, poor health becomes the outcome of material deprivation. Whilst, for example, nutrition may be an important etiological factor in ill-health, the focus would be on factors that influence a person's ability to make choices about the food they buy. It has been calculated that a healthy diet, as defined in the National Advisory Council on Nutrition Education report could cost up to 35 per cent more than the typical diet of a low income family (Whitehead, 1987).

Table 6.8 presents data of household expenditure as a function of household type and income level in 1985. From this it is evident that low income households consistently spend a higher

TABLE 6.8 *Weekly food expenditure as a function of weekly household income*

Household			
	£ inc per week	% on food	£ on food
Low income	61	26	15.86
Mid income	151	21	31.71
High income	297	17	50.49

Adapted from *Social Trends* (1988).

proportion of their income on food than middle or high income households. However, in real terms the actual amount they are able to spend on food is significantly less. For example, if we take all households; those in the low income bracket spend 26 per cent of their total weekly income (£60.70) which amounts to £15.85 on food. High income households spend only 17 per cent of their income on food and yet this amounts to £50.49 per week.

The Black Report found in the light of the extensive evidence the working group had considered, the materialist explanation of health inequalities was the most viable. Subsequently *The Health Divide* found:

> Fresh evidence (which) shows that life-style and material living conditions influence health and vary with occupational class. Furthermore, recent in-depth studies have increased understanding of how living and working conditions impose severe restrictions on an individual's ability to choose a healthy life style. They have provided fresh insight into the way behaviours are influenced by social conditions and argue for a policy which recognises the link between the two, in preference to policies which focus solely on the individual.

How the evidence on inequalities and health are interpreted has important implications for health policy and for decision making in terms of the allocation of financial resources and the types of provision for health that are required. Like the findings of the epidemiologists we described earlier in this chapter, it would seem that any real attempt to improve health lies beyond health care as it has been traditionally conceived and must address wider social issues.

Further Reading

Doyal, L. (1983) *The Political Economy of Health*, London, Pluto Press.
McKeown, T. (1979) *The Role of Medicine*, Oxford, Blackwell.
Mitchell, J. (1984) *What is to be done about Health and Illness?* Harmondsworth, Penguin. Chapter One.
Rathwell, T. and Phillips, D. (eds.) (1986) *Health, Race and Ethnicity*, Croom Helm, London.
Townsend, P. and Davidson, N. (1982) *Inequalities in Health: The Black Report*, Harmondsworth, Penguin.

Whitehead, M. (1987) *The Health Divide: Inequalities in the 1980's*, London, Health Education Council.

References

Black, J. and Laws, S. (1986) *Living with Sickle Cell Disease*, London, Sickle Cell Society.

Blane, D. (1985) An Assessment of the Black Report's Explanation of Health Inequalities, *Sociology of Health and Illness*, 7: 423–445.

Donovan, J. (1984) Ethnicity and Health: a Research Review, *Social Science and Medicine*, 19: 663–670.

Fagin, L. (1984) *The Forsaken Families: the Effects of Unemployment on Family Life*, Harmondsworth, Penguin.

Gershuny, J. (1983) *Social Innovation and the Division of Labour*, Oxford, Oxford University Press.

Goldberg, E. M. and Morrison, S. L. (1963) Schizophrenia and Social Class, *British Journal of Psychiatry*, 109: 785–802.

Graham, H. (1984) *Women, Health and the Family*, Brighton, Wheatsheaf Books.

Illsley, R. (1986) Occupational Class Selection and the Production of Inequalities in Health, *Quarterly Journal of Social Affairs*, 2: 151–165.

Joelson, L. and Wahlquist, L. (1987) The Psychological Meaning of Job Insecurity and Job Loss: Results of a Longitudinal Study, *Social Science and Medicine*, 25: 179–182.

Littlewood, R. and Cross, S. (1980) Ethnic Minorities and Psychiatric services, *Sociology of Health and Illness*, 2: 2.

Maclure, A, Stewart, G. T. (1984) Admissions of Children to Hospital in Glasgow: Relation to Unemployment and Other Deprivation Variables, *Lancet* ii: 682–688.

Marmot, G. G., Adelstein, A. M. and Bulusu, L. (1984) Immigrant Mortality in England and Wales, *Population Trends*, London, HMSO.

Marmott, M. and Theorell, T. (1988) Social Class and Cardiovascular Disease: The Contribution of Work, *International Journal of Health Services*, 18: 659–674.

Meredith Davies, J. B. (1983) *Community Health, Preventative Medicine and Social Services*, London, Bailliere Tindall.

OPCS (1982) Mortality Statistics 1978, London, HMSO.

OPCS (1986) Registrar General's Decennial Supplement on Occupational mortality 1979–1983, London, HMSO.

Rathwell, T. and Phillips, D. (eds.) (1986) *Health, Race and Ethnicity*, London, Croom Helm.

Social Trends (1988) London, HMSO.

Thompson, E. P. (1977) *The Making of the English Working Class*, Harmondsworth, Penguin.

Thunhurst, C. (1985) *Poverty and Health in the City of Sheffield*, Environmental Health Dept. Sheffield City Council.

Townsend, P. and Davidson, N. (1982) *Inequalities in Health: the Black Report*, Harmondsworth, Penguin.

Townsend, P., Phillimore, P., and Beattie, A. (1986) *Inequalities· in Health in the Northern Region: an Interim Report*, Northern Regional Health Authority and the University of Bristol.

Wadsworth, M. E. J. (1986) Serious Illness in Childhood and its Association with Later Life Achievements, in Wilkinson R.G. (ed.) *Class and Health: Research and Longitudinal Data*, London, Tavistock.

Waldron, I. (1983) Sex Differences in Illness Incidence, Prognosis and Mortality: Issues and Evidence, *Social Science and Medicine*, 17: 1107–1123.

Whitehead, M. (1987) *The Health Divide: Inequalities in the 1980s*, London, Health Education Council.

7 Is Pharmacy a Profession?

In addressing the question 'is pharmacy a profession?' it will first be necessary to appreciate what we mean by the term profession. This chapter aims to offer such an appreciation. When reading this chapter, it will be beneficial to reflect upon what it means to be a pharmacist, what it means to be a health professional, what is the position of pharmacists within the community and what is their relationship with other health workers.

There is an extensive literature on the sociology of the professions and there is considerable debate over what actually constitutes a profession. Certain attributes, however, are generally accepted as distinguishing a profession. Some occupations, in particular those of law and medicine, have acquired a pre-eminent status in our society and have become institutions with a great deal of prestige and power. This distinguishes them from other occupations. For these occupations the term professional has an important sociological meaning, one which is different from its more colloquial sense. For example, when we speak of professional footballers we imply that they are skilled and are payed to play their chosen sport, but they do not possess the key characteristics which define a profession in the sociological sense. Let us look at the features that define a profession and then turn to consider whether or not pharmacy can be considered a profession.

7.1 SOCIOLOGICAL APPROACHES TO PROFESSIONALISATION

The question why some occupations rise to the status of profession whilst others do not is a sociological puzzle calling for an explanation. Since Parsons published his paper, 'The Professions and the Social Structure' in 1939 many theories have been postulated. Until the 1970s most writers tried to explain the professions' unique position in society by way of definitions. That is, they tried to identify or define those characteristics of an occupation which were special or peculiar to professional status. This resulted in

73

a proliferation of literature listing the professions' attributes, for example, Goode (1960). This has been referred to as the 'attribute' or the 'trait' approach.

The following traits have been most frequently identified:

1. A profession determines its own standards of education and training.
2. The student professional undergoes an extensive training and socialisation process.
3. Professional practice is legally recognised by some form of licensure.
4. Licensing and admission boards are run by members of the profession.
5. Most legislation which affects a profession is shaped by that profession.
6. A profession gains in income, power and status and can demand higher calibre students.
7. The professional is relatively free from lay evaluation.
8. The norms of practice enforced by the profession are often more stringent than legal controls.
9. Members of a profession have a powerful sense of identification and affiliation with their occupational group.
10. A profession is more likely to remain a life-time occupation.

Rather than attempting to simply define the attributes of professions, some sociologists have suggested that professions have achieved their importance or status because they carried out functions which were vital to the workings of modern industrialised society. Sociologists refer to this as the 'functionalist explanation'; it views society as an organism in which all the parts function in a way that ensures the continued well-being of the whole organism, rather like the various physiological systems of the human body. All social institutions have a use, otherwise they would cease to have a function and would quickly disappear. Complex industrial societies need expert knowledge, and professions perform the function of applying their expert knowledge for the benefit of the community. Whilst both the trait and functional approaches have since been surpassed by more critical and realistic analyses, we can begin to appreciate that professions (a) possess certain important characteristics or traits, and (b) fulfil important societal functions.

7.2 CORE FEATURES OF A PROFESSION

Certain 'core' features have been identified that are possessed by all professions. These can be summarised as:

1. Specialised knowledge and lengthy training.
2. Service orientation.
3. Monopoly of practice.
4. Self-regulation.

To become accepted into a profession an individual must undergo a period of training. This is invariably long (for example seven years for architecture, five years for medicine) and highly specialised. This high degree of training is required, because the professional must possess a specialised knowledge which is not readily accessible to the rest of the population. In many ways it is this specialised knowledge that sets professionals apart from the lay person who does not possess such knowledge or expertise. Consequently the lay person is reliant on the 'expert's' service. Indeed a second characteristic of a profession is service orientation – this means that professionals should work in the best interests of their clients. Professionals should not be intent on pursuing their self interest. This characteristic is very important because a profession has a monopoly of practice in its given field. This monopoly is granted and secured by the state. In other words, it is illegal for people other than members of the profession to carry out defined tasks; for example, it is illegal for anyone other than a qualified surgeon to carry out a heart transplant.

In addition to the restriction of practice, a profession monitors or 'polices' itself. Freidson (1970a) argues that a profession is 'distinct from other occupations in that it has been given the right to control its own work'. A profession regulates the system of training, decides who is eligible to enter the profession and assesses who is competent to practise within the profession. That is to say, they 'self-regulate'. Professionals maintain that the unusual degree of skill and knowledge involved in professional activities means that non-professionals are not properly equipped to evaluate or regulate the professions' activities. If a professional does not perform competently or ethically, his or her peers preside over the outcome; they are constituted as a professional body. In the case of medicine in the UK, this is the General Medical Council.

It is often claimed that professions as social institutions wield power and influence, in that to a great extent most legislation that affects a profession is shaped by that profession itself. Currently, the 'restrictive practices ' of the professions are under review and through the introduction of certain mechanisms they are becoming more accountable to other than themselves. An example of this was the amendment to the NHS Regulations (1985) by the Health Minister, Kenneth Clark, in April 1985. This amendment, known as the 'Limited List', restricted the medicinal products of a particular class such as, cough remedies and benzodiazepines, for which the NHS would pay. This was attacked by both the pharmaceutical industry and the medical profession as an encroachment on the clinical judgement and a restriction of the clinical freedom of general practitioners.

The notion of professional judgement is an important one in any discussion of professions. This is because, in order to remain exclusive to the members of the profession itself, its work must not become routinised or rationalised. Professionals, as a result of their training, have acquired the ability to make assessments or judgements on the basis of experience and skill. Jamous and Peloille (1970) have described this in terms of the 'I/T' ratio, that is, the profession has claims to greater indeterminate knowledge (I) than technical knowledge (T). Indeterminate knowledge is personal knowledge and personal judgement, whilst technical knowledge refers to knowledge that is rational and codified. Similarly, Freidson, in his book *Professional Dominance*, (1970b), called this the 'clinical mentality'. He distinguished the medical practitioner (the clinician) from the scientist or theorist. The clinician's primary orientation is towards action, to an extent that he or she may prefer to do something with very uncertain chances of success than do nothing at all. The practitioner, Freidson argues, 'believes what he is doing', i.e. professionals are likely to display personal commitment to their chosen course of action. The practitioner is essentially a pragmatist, relying on results rather than theory, trusting personal rather than book knowledge. It may be pertinent to consider whether pharmacists are clinicians or scientists.

7.3   THE PROCESS OF PROFESSIONALISATION

The paramedical professions, for example nursing and physiotherapy, are in a different position from the medical profession, for while it is legitimate for them to take orders from, and be assessed by, physicians, it is not legitimate for them to give orders or evaluate the work of doctors. Hence while they possess many of the attributes of a profession, in that there is a system of registration and licensing, and formal standards of training together with regulation of their own members, they do not enjoy the full autonomy of a profession.

We have so far assumed that what constitutes a profession is dependent on something special or superior about a particular occupation; their possession of knowledge and skills that ensures that they have total control over a particular sphere of work. However, whilst the length of training, service orientation, code of ethics and expertise are all significant in persuading the state and the public of their importance, they are not 'causes' of an occupation achieving professional status nor, it would seem, are they objectively determined attributes. Wright (1979) in his paper, 'A Study of the Legitimisation of Knowledge: the success of medicine, the failure of astrology', has illustrated this point. He argues that the success of medicine as a profession is not because of anything intrinsic in medical knowledge. Indeed when physicians first began to organise themselves into groups, there was no evidence that their knowledge and methods were any more effective than those of astrologists. The differences lay rather in the social position of doctors, the social position of their clients and, ultimately, their success in legitimising their activities.

This sociological perspective then, views the process of professionalisation as one of occupational control; and professional autonomy is seen to be the outcome of the interaction between political and economic powers, and occupational representation, which is often helped by educational institutions that persuade the state that the occupation's work is reliable and valuable. That is to say, occupations achieve their status as professions as the result of political struggles and power conflicts between different interest groups. An occupation becomes a profession not so much because of improvements in its skills and knowledge, but rather because the profession's leaders are successful in convincing the state that autonomy and self regulation are desirable. It may not then be the characteristics of professionals per se that determine their status so much as their relationships with clients, and other occupations. This perspective has been developed by Johnson in his book, *Professions and Power* (1989). Johnson rejects the 'trait' theory of professionalism as inadequate. Instead of pondering the question whether an occupation is a profession, it may be more appropriate to consider the circumstances in which individuals attempt to turn an occupation into a profession. It has been suggested that,

> this line of approach avoids many of the pitfalls opened up by frankly evaluating definitions of the professions. It concentrates upon determining circumstances under which occupational groups make an avowal of professionalism and leaves to others the task of judging how close they come to living up to the professional. (King, 1968; quoted by Johnson, 1989)

How successful an occupation's claim to professionalism is depends in part on the power relationship between the occupation's members and those served by them. An important element of this relationship, Johnson observes, is that of 'mystification'. Members of an occupation which aspires to professional status may only achieve their aim in circumstances whereby they are able to successfully promote their services as esoteric. In creating a dependence upon their skills, members of such occupations reduce the areas of knowledge and experience they have in common with those they serve. This increase in the 'social distance' between themselves and their clients provides professionals with an opportunity for autonomous control over their practices. In other words, by promoting the esoteric nature of their services, professionals ward off potential challenges to their status from the lay public. Hence it is not simply a list of attributes that define a profession, rather the public's willingness to accept or their inability to successfully challenge the professionals' area of expertise.

7.4   THE EMERGENCE OF PHARMACY

The preparation of medicines has occurred throughout history. The earliest records date from the second millennium BC, and this practice occurred in the ancient civilisations of Egypt, Babylonia, Asia, Greece and Rome. In Britain during the Middle Ages, people having similar business interests or crafts grouped themselves together into craft or merchant guilds. In the fourteenth century the Company of Grocers of London was formed, of which apothecaries formed a sub-group. Two centuries later, the Society of Apothecaries was founded, and a subsequent Royal Charter established the apothecaries' monopoly in the dispensing of medicines against physicians' prescriptions, whilst members of the Company of Grocers retained the right to sell drugs and spices and later became known as 'druggists'. During the sixteenth century, people who were unable to either reach or afford a physician went to an apothecary for diagnosis, advice and supply of medicines.

Dispensing within the dispensary established by the College of Physicians in 1696 was performed by assistants, who were either druggists or apprentices to apothecaries. These later became known as 'dispensing chemists'. Thus by the eighteenth century three rival groups were involved in the compounding and dispensing of medicines, namely the apothecaries, druggists and dispensing chemists. In 1841 the Pharmaceutical Society of Great Britain was founded and incorporated by Royal Charter in 1843. The Society was founded to represent the interests of chemists and druggists, to raise their profile amongst the professions and to promote education and training. The Pharmacy Acts (1852 and 1868) restricted titles such as 'Pharmaceutical Chemist' and 'Pharmacist' to those registered with the Society, although membership was optional.

Since the Pharmacy and Poisons Act (1933) membership of the Pharmaceutical Society, together with the registration of premises has been required for all persons engaged in the selling or dispensing of listed poisons and controlled medicines. The premises should at all times be under the personal control of a pharmacist. In 1988 the Pharmaceutical Society was renamed the Royal Pharmaceutical Society of Great Britain.

7.5 PHARMACY AS A PROFESSION

Pharmacy as an occupation would appear to exhibit a number of characteristics suggested as features of a profession as defined by the 'trait' theory.

1. Monopoly of practice

Currently, membership of the Royal Pharmaceutical Society is restricted to persons registered as Pharmaceutical Chemists under

the terms of the Pharmacy Act, 1954. This act restricts entry to the
Register of Pharmaceutical Chemists to those who have attained a
degree in pharmacy at an approved School of Pharmacy, or who
have passed the Pharmaceutical Chemist Qualifying Examination,
provided they have paid the necessary fees, are at least 21 years
of age and have completed subsequent to passing a final degree
examination not less than one year of pre-registration training in
an approved establishment. Thus since 1954, pharmacists have
had, with a very few exceptions, i.e. dispensing doctors, a state-
legitimised monopoly over compounding and dispensing drugs. In
addition, pharmacists have a monopoly over the sale of 'Pharmacy
Medicines'.

2. Specialised knowledge and lengthy training

The undergraduate pharmacy degree course lasts three or four
years and is followed by one year of pre-registration training (with
the exception of Bradford University which offers a four year sand-
wich course including two six month periods of pre-registration
training). Upon successful completion of this extensive period of
training, pharmacists have unique knowledge and skills relating to
the preparation and clinical applications of drug use.

3. Service orientation

Pharmacists provide a range of pharmaceutical services including
the supply of medicines and appliances, treatment of minor ailments, and the provision of health care advice.

4. Self-regulation

The Pharmacy and Poisons Act (1933) created the Statutory Committee of the Pharmaceutical Society. This Committee, comprising
mainly pharmacists and having a chairman 'having practical, legal
experience', appointed by the Privy Council, acts as the discipli-
nary body for members of the pharmaceutical profession.

Therefore application of the 'trait' approach would seem to indicate that pharmacy may indeed be considered a profession. However, it is a matter of debate as to whether or not the full autonomy

of pharmacy as a profession has been achieved (Turner, 1987; Shuval, 1981).

Three factors hinder the professional autonomy of the pharmacist: (a) commercialism; (b) the increase of commercial pharmaceutical formulation and packaging; (c) dependence on physicians.

The majority (73 per cent) of pharmacists practise in the community (see Chapter 2). The commercial interests necessary in successfully running a business may seem to be at odds with the ethos of impartial service orientation. The provision of resources for health care is limited, and, like other scarce commodities they should be used economically. Examples of this are the trend towards generic prescribing by general practitioners, and proposals for making general practitioners more responsible for their budgets (Department of Health, 1989).

The increased availability of pre-formulated medicines and the emergence of original-pack dispensing means that the time taken to dispense medicines is less than in the past. Consequently, the 'mystique' the public has traditionally associated with the compounding aspects of the pharmacist's role has largely disappeared. As we have seen in chapter two, these changes in the nature of dispensing have not necessarily resulted in a lessened role for pharmacists in the dispensing process. However, as we have illustrated, the criteria for professional status depends on the profession maintaining a 'social distance' from the public it serves, and nowadays the pharmacist may appear to the public to be merely a counter of tablets and supplier of prepackaged medicines.

The pharmacist, to a great extent, receives his/her directions from the physician. It is the physician who makes the assessment of the case from a clinical and therapeutic viewpoint, and the pharmacist dispenses in accordance with the prescriber's wishes. Both in the hospital and the community environment the pharmacist is 'governed' by the decisions and judgements of the medical profession.

These two factors – the increased use of prepackaged medicines, and the dependence of pharmacists on the doctor's judgement – it could be argued, have contributed to a shift in the pharmaceutical profession's I/T ratio in that there is limited scope for the pharmacist to bring their own unique knowledge and skills to their day-to-day tasks; that is to say, they are too highly trained for the jobs they do. Turner (1987) has argued that the knowledge base in pharmacy is very specialised and precise and hence lacks a certain degree of mystique in contrast to the 'clinical mentality' whereby doctors constantly make decisions in the face of uncertainty.

Currently there are some important questions to be asked about the nature of pharmacists' activities and their contribution to the provision of health care. This will have implications for their relationships with other health professionals as well as their relationships with consumers of health care. Opportunities exist for pharmacists to develop professional skills in addition to those with which they have been traditionally associated. By taking on the 'extended role' as outlined previously, the opportunity exists for pharmacists to shed the image of over-educated health workers. This would in turn have the effect of increasing pharmacists' I/T ratio, i.e. as pharmacists become increasingly involved in providing health care advice and education, there will be a commensurate rise in their level of indeterminate knowledge. This development should enhance pharmacy's claims to full professional status.

Further Reading

Johnson, T. (1989) *Professions and Power*, London, Macmillan Education Ltd.

Turner, B. S. (1987) *Medical Power and Social Knowledge*, London, Sage Publications Ltd. Chapter Seven.

References

Department of Health (1989) *Working for Patients*, (Cmd 555), London, HMSO.

Freidson, E. (1970a) *Profession of Medicine; A Study in the Sociology of Applied Knowledge*, New York, Dodd, Mead and Co.

Freidson, E. (1970b) *Professional Dominance*, Chicago, Atherton Press.

Goode, W. J. (1960) Encroachment, Charlatanism and the Emerging Profession: psychiatry, sociology and medicine, *American Sociological Review*, 25: 902–914.

Jamous, H. and Peloille, B. (1970) Changes in the French University Hospital System, in Jackson J. A. (ed.) *Professions and Professionalisation*, Cambridge, Cambridge University Press.

Johnson, T. (1989) *Professions and Power*, London, Macmillan Education Ltd.

King, M. D. (1968) Science and the Professional Dilemma, in Gould J. (ed.), *Penguin Social Sciences Survey, 1968,* Harmondsworth, Penguin.

Parsons, T. (1939) The Professions and the Social Structure, *Social Forces,* 17: 457–467.

Shuval, J. T. (1981) The Contribution of Psychology and Social Phenomena to an Understanding of the Aetiology of Disease and Illness, *Social Science and Medicine,* 15: 337–342.

The National Health Service (General Medical and Pharmaceutical Services) Amendment Regulations 1985.

Turner, B. S. (1987) *Medical Power and Social Knowledge,* London, Sage Publications Ltd.

Wright, P. (1979) A Study of the Legitimisation of Knowledge: the Success of Medicine, the Failure of Astrology, in Wallis R. (ed.) *On the Margins of Science,* Sociological Review Monograph 27, Keele.

8 Health Education and Health Promotion

It is now recognised that many people take positive action to preserve their health, which is not simply a matter of responding to symptoms. Consequently it can be argued that it is now more appropriate to speak in terms of 'health behaviour' rather than 'illness behaviour'. In their book, *Sociological Approaches to Health and Medicine*, Morgan *et al.* (1985) defined health behaviour as: '. . . behaviour in relation to the adoption of officially recommended health actions, such as following a 'healthy' diet, giving up smoking, or using preventive services.'

The community pharmacist, it could be argued, is well placed to offer opportunistic health education and health promotion to the public. However, educating people about aspects of preventive health and encouraging them to act upon this information is a complex process. In this chapter we examine a number of approaches to health education and consider some of the obstacles the health educator faces in attempting to promote healthy lifestyles.

8.1 HEALTH POLICY AND HEALTH EDUCATION

In recent decades illness prevention has become a major priority in health policy. This has been the result of a combination of factors, including a growing appreciation of the limitations of conventional medical practice (see Chapter 5) and an increasing concern about the rapidly increasing costs of health care services and the insatiable demand for health care (Klein, 1983). Implicit in the strategy of health education, which encourages people to take responsibility for the maintenance and preservation of their own health, was the hope that there would be a subsequent reduction in demand for services. Successive governments have been eager to adopt a preventative approach to health care. These have been outlined in a series of government documents detailing the merits of preventative health strategies (DHSS, 1976a, 1976b, 1976/77).

Two major themes run through these reports. First, they recognised the need to reduce the demands on public spending and second, there was an emphasis on the contribution individuals could make to improving their own health status. For example, the 1977 sub-committee of the parliamentary expenditure committee stated 'the sub-committee was particularly interested in the prevalence of disease precipitated by individuals' (Klein, 1983). The Government also argued that while there was plenty of scope for preventative action involving substantial expenditure, there were also possibilities for the introduction of measures which would not require large financial resources, and emphasised the contribution that the individual could make to prevention (DHSS, 1976a, 1976b).

Whilst preventive measures are generally considered to be desirable, the approach to prevention and health has been the focus of much debate. Health policy has increasingly emphasised the value of prevention rather than cure and has largely focused on individual lifestyles. This strategy has caused a great deal of controversy and has been challenged by those who argue that it fails to address the real determinants of health, which are seen to lie in social and economic factors. Poverty, poor housing and food policies, for example, would seem to be more important considerations in promoting health than 'healthy eating' or taking 'regular exercise'.

The circumstances which permit or enable people to live healthy lives are an essential prerequisite to healthy lifestyles. In other words, the divergent approaches to preventative health policy are closely allied to our interpretation or explanation of the relationship between social factors and health (Chapter 6). For instance, to assume that everyone can adopt a healthy lifestyle, i.e. partake of a balanced diet, sufficient exercise and so forth, fails to take into account the individuals' immediate circumstances and the environment in which they live, which may actually prevent the adoption of such lifestyles.

8.2 DEFINING PREVENTION

At this point, it may be useful to define what we mean by prevention in relation to ill-health. In health policy, it is generally accepted that there are three levels or dimensions to prevention.

1. Primary Prevention: action to prevent the occurrence of disease or disability, for example immunisation and vaccination, improved sanitation, water fluoridisation, better housing and nutrition. Within the National Health Service, services mainly concerned with primary prevention include family planning, immunisation schemes, health education and health visiting. Examples of health prevention outside the NHS would include clean-air acts, seat-belt legislation, environmental health, health and safety at work act, and the factory inspectorate.
2. Secondary Prevention: the early detection of a condition which if detected may be treated. This form of preventive activity may include dental examinations, eye testing, periodic medical examinations, and screening techniques, for example, blood pressure measuring, blood-glucose and cholesterol testing, and cervical smears.
3. Tertiary Prevention: minimising disability arising out of existing conditions. This may involve care or rehabilitation for conditions such as hearing impairment, diabetes, epilepsy, mental disorder and spinal injuries.

The increasing emphasis on prevention has significant implications for the health professions. The government has repeatedly pointed to the contribution that health professionals can make to health prevention and health promotion. Both the Government White Paper *Promoting Better Health* and the Nuffield Enquiry into Pharmacy envisaged an extended role for pharmacists as health promoters, involving the dissemination of information, literature and advice to patients, for example. It is acknowledged that the community pharmacist is well placed to provide health information and health education (McEwan, 1983) and it is significant that a patient will see a pharmacist consistently more frequently than any other health professional (Morrow, *et al.*, 1986).

Before discussing the more specific implications for pharmacists in chapter nine, let us first consider what is understood by the terms 'health education' and 'health promotion' and reflect briefly on the philosophy underlying health education.

8.3 DEFINING HEALTH EDUCATION

It is possible to identify three aspects of health education. First there is education about the human body and how to look after it. Second there is education about the health services and information about their availability and use. Third there is consideration of the wider environment, where information can be disseminated and changes effected with respect to matters such as pollution and clean water.

Health education has been defined in many ways. The definition offered by Catford and Nutbeam (1984) is instructive: Health education '. . . seeks to improve or protect health through voluntary changes in behaviour as a consequence of learning opportunities. It can include personal education and development, and mass media information and education'. In other words, the aim of health educators would be to encourage people to change their behaviour and adopt healthy activities with a view to improving their health status. Education can take place at personal, community, and societal levels.

Tones (1986) has identified three approaches to health education. All are still practised to a greater or lesser extent. The order in which they are presented here reflects the historical development of approaches to health education.

1. Traditional Health Education
   The traditional health education approach is based on the belief that the incidence of ill-health can be reduced considerably if individuals adopt a healthy lifestyle. Health education has therefore been traditionally designed to persuade individuals to replace their unhealthy patterns of behaviour with mostly healthy ones. Hence the task of health educators has been, for example, to persuade people to drink less alcohol, stop smoking, and reduce their consumption of animal fats, on the grounds that doing so would promote their health. This approach has obvious financial attractions for health educators in so far as the savings made by a reduction in demand for health care services would far outweigh the cost of a persuasive health education campaign.

2. 'Educational Model'
   The educational model of health education is less didactic in approach. Its underlying principle is that individuals should be educated, not about specific health issues, but about decision-making skills, in order that individuals may make informed choices about their health related behaviour.

However, as Tones argues, this model is not without its critics. The impact of socialisation may mean that a rational decision competes with cultural influences in making decisions. For instance, individuals 'addicted' to drugs may be fully aware of the risks to their health from drug misuse, but may not be in a position to stop their drug-taking because of the social milieu in which they live (Harding, 1988). Similarly, an adolescent's decision to smoke may be made by reference to cultural or peer decision making processes which 'rationalise' smoking as 'tough' 'glamorous' or even 'a stimulant' to help cope with living in a dreary environment. Failure to make the rational choice – to give up smoking for health reasons – can lead to a situation of 'victim blaming' by health educators, as individuals are blamed for failing to make the 'required' health-promoting decisions.

3. 'Radical Model'
    A much broader approach to health education is advocated by the 'radical model'. As we have already discussed in chapter six, ill-health is not simply a matter of bad luck, but is related to social factors. An assumption of the 'radical model' is that individuals can be emancipated from potential ill-health. This may be achieved first by raising their awareness of the obstacles to health, and second, by individuals taking positive action against these obstacles. For example, air pollution from heavy industrial processing plants situated next to a residential area may be a significant contributor to a high local incidence of chest diseases. The 'radical' model advocates that people become aware of the adverse effects of such an industry on their health, and encourages concerned individuals to take collective action against the cause of ill-health. In essence, then, this model is 'radical' in that it attempts to make health education a political issue by encouraging people to use their collective power to promote health.

The limitations of the 'traditional' or 'educational' approach to health education have been clearly articulated by Rodmell and Watt in their book *The Politics of Health Education* (1986). They have challenged the traditional health education approach on five counts.

1. Traditional health education 'individualises' health – that is,

the preservation of health is considered by health educators as the responsibility of the individual.

2. 'Elitism' – an implicit assumption of the traditional health education philosophy is an absence or inappropriateness of the lay person's own health knowledge. Thus health educators may assume that their interpretation of health and illness is better or more appropriate than the interpretation of lay people. Consequently health education programmes can be insensitive to socio-cultural variations in health knowledge, or ride rough shod over them.

3. Health education is frequently imposed on individuals without the message being tailored to their need, that is, they may not be told what they want or need to know, but rather what the education programme wants to teach. Moreover, failure to pick up on this inappropriate health education message is often deemed to be the result of the recipient's irresponsibility or intransigence.

4. The dominant value system in society is used as a vehicle to promote health. That is, health education like media advertising, relies on the use of images. These images, however, are frequently reflections of affluent, white, middle-class life styles. The values implicit in these images may be totally unrelated to or divorced from the lifestyles of the targeted audience.

5. The agenda for health education is not always determined strictly in accordance with health needs. The agenda is drawn up on the basis of political decisions about the allocation of scarce financial resources, and this agenda may be drafted by individuals whose life experiences may be far removed from, and have little in common with, the targeted population.

8.4 DEFINING HEALTH PROMOTION

It is important that health professionals who are being encouraged to participate more actively in health education are aware of what is involved at both a practical and philosophical level. Simply telling health professionals to become health educators can be counterproductive for both the consumers and providers of health care. For instance, a study of community dental practitioners found that their attempts to deliver health education within the context of the dental surgery resulted in the dentists feeling that they were inadequate and ineffective. Moreover, patients receiving dental health advice felt guilty when they failed to live up to the dentist's expectations in terms of their diet and oral hygiene (Nettleton, 1986, 1989).

Health promotion involves the various means which enable or facilitate people to preserve and/or maintain their health. Catford and Nutbeam (1984) define health promotion as that which 'seeks to improve or protect health through behavioural, biological, socio-economical and environmental changes. It can include health education, personal services, environmental measures, community and organisational development and economic regulatory activities'. Health promotion is more than dissemination of information and would involve attempts to influence the activities of employers and local authorities, for example.

The literature on health promotion and pharmacy is as yet limited, in that health education has been conceived primarily in terms of advice giving in response to the presentation of symptoms. More, however, has been written on opportunistic health education and health promotion in relation to medical general practice. A particularly instructive paper is Watt's 'Community Health Initiatives and their Relationship to General Practice' (1986). Watt points to the development and proliferation of community health initiatives. She notes that 12 000 community initiatives are known to exist in the United Kingdom. These initiatives fall into three categories:

1. Self-help groups, where, 'people who either suffer from a condition or are relatives of a sufferer, meet together to give each other mutual support'.
2. Community-help groups are locally based groups which recognise and address the importance of social factors to health. Watt gives the following example: 'Women on a housing estate who share a state of depression, and who identify its cause as isolation which in turn is caused by there being nowhere safe for small children to play, decide to treat the depression by campaigning for play space'.
3. Community development health projects are usually local authority funded projects which are focused on a specific health issue. The principle aim is to encourage and facilitate participation in that people should have a far greater say in the

conditions in which they live. 'While community development health projects vary widely, one common element is the understanding that health is not an individual matter. Participants in community development health projects identify the causes of ill health in certain social factors over which individuals have little control.'

Watt suggests that there is scope for useful links to be formed between these initiatives and general practitioners, and she offers suggestions as to how general practitioners may contribute to community health schemes. These suggestions are worthy of consideration by other health care professionals. In particular, pharmacists who are community-based may well be in a position to contribute to such health promotion initiatives. Suggestions which may be of particular relevance for community pharmacists include:

1. Taking into consideration patients' own experiences, interpretations, and perceived health needs may enable health practitioners to offer more effective support.
2. Health practitioners should be aware of and become involved in 'local informal health networks'. For example, the community health council, the council for voluntary service, and local self-help groups.
3. Health practitioners might serve as a resource for community-based groups, for example offering to give informal talks to such groups.

8.5 SOCIOLOGICAL APPROACHES TO HEALTH EDUCATION

Medical sociologists have identified two divergent approaches to health education. These approaches reflect the two models of health and illness outlined in chapter five. One approach assumes that the individual can be held totally responsible for his or her own behaviour, while the other recognises that there are social constraints on the individual's actions. Such constraints have been reported in a study of health care routines in the family by Graham (1984), who makes a distinction between health choices and health compromises. The notion of choice is one that is central to health education. The theory is that, when given information and advice, for example on diet, smoking or exercise, people are placed in a position to choose whether or not to follow that advice. In practice, however, her research revealed that the idea of being able to choose was often unrealistic and that responding to such advice meant having to make compromises, that is, individuals weigh up the costs and benefits of responding to a health education message.

Bewley *et al.* (1984) in a study of adolescent attitudes to illness and health identified a number of social and health care problems experienced by young people living in an inner city area. Family disharmony compounded by poor housing and a lack of educational and employment opportunities were frequently reported by young people as among some of the problems they faced, and 'getting away' was considered the best solution. This situation, Bewley noted, illustrates the inappropriateness of the didactic approach of traditional health education, which fails to take into account the target audience's socio-economic environment. Many of Bewley's respondents were aware of the chances they were taking with their health, but they were not prepared to do anything about some risks, such as smoking. From their own perspective preventive health behaviour was relegated to a low place on their list of priorities, as they continued to live in an environment where coping with the daily problems of inner city life were given uppermost priority.

Similar findings to Bewley's, which confirm that people's health beliefs are rooted in the social and economic fabric of their everyday lives, are reported in Farrant and Russell's study of the utilisation of health education publications (1985). They relate evidence which suggests that people who behave in ways damaging to their health do so not directly out of ignorance or a lack of motivation. Instead there are a multiplicity of factors which influence people's health and illness behaviour (Chapter 3). Researchers argue that the failure to bridge the persistent gap between the messages of health education and their implementation lies less with individuals and more with the social structure in which they live.

The limitations that this imposes on the scope of traditional forms of health education are formidable. A way of acknowledging these limitations is to take account of, and draw upon, people's previous health experiences. That is to say, the way people define their state of health is through drawing on past knowledge and experience of health and illness, as discussed in chapter three. For instance, in response to a patient requesting excessive quantities of laxatives the pharmacist may recommend an increase in the intake of dietary fibre. This advice, although therapeutically sound, may be inadequate as it takes no account of the patient's personal and social circumstances, for example, who purchases the food in his or her household, how much money is available for food, the time available for purchase and preparation of food, food preferences of the patient and family, their existing health beliefs – for example their traditionally held beliefs on the merits of laxatives. All these factors come into play in the process of health promotion.

So it can been seen that there are two approaches to health education which differ in their emphasis. These are not mutually exclusive. It is important that pharmacists' policy and practice of health education fully appreciates that it is inadequate to merely provide information in a didactic manner, on the assumption that all individuals will respond in the same way. Rather, a health promotion policy should reflect an awareness of the attitudes, values and circumstances of those people at whom the policy is aimed.

Further Reading

Rodmell, S. and Watt, A. (1986) *The Politics of Health Education: Raising the Issues*, London, Routledge and Kegan Paul.

References

Bewley, B. R., Higgs, R. H. and Jones, A. (1984) Adolescent Patients in an Inner London General Practice: Their Attitudes to Illness and Health Care, *Journal of the Royal College of General Practitioners*, 34: 543–546.

Catford, J. and Nutbeam, D. (1984) Towards a Definition of Health Education and Health Promotion, *Health Education Journal*, 43: 38.

DHSS (1976a) *Priorities for Health and Personal Social Services in England*, London, HMSO.

DHSS (1976b) *Prevention and Health: Everybody's Business: A Reassessment of Public and Personal Health*, London, HMSO.

DHSS (1976/77) *First Report from the Expenditure Committee, session 1976/77 Preventative Medicine Volume 1 Report*, London, HMSO.

Farrant, W. and Russell, J. (1985) *Health Education Council Publications: A Case Study in the Production, Distribution and Use of Health Information*. Final Report of the Health Education Publications Project, Institute of Education, University of London.

Graham, H. (1984) *Women, Health and the Family*, Brighton, Wheatsheaf Books.

Harding, G. (1988) Patterns of Heroin Use: What Do We Know? *British Journal of Addiction*, 83: 1247–1254.

Klein, R. (1983) *The Politics of the National Health Service*, London, Longman.

McEwan, J. (1983), Pharmacy in Inner City Areas: Opportunities for Health Education, *Pharmaceutical Journal*, 231: 346–348.

Morgan, M., Calnan, M. and Manning, N. (1985) *Sociological Approaches to Health and Illness*, London, Routledge and Kegan Paul.

Morrow, N. C., Speedy, P. and Totten, C. (1986) Health Education Perspectives in Continuing Education Programmes for Pharmacists, *Health Education Journal*, 45: 166–170.

Nettleton, S. J. (1986) Understanding Dental Health Beliefs: An Introduction to Ethnography, *British Dental Journal*, 161: 145–147.

Nettleton S. J. (1989) Dentists and Dental Health Education: a Study of the Perceptions of 28 Community Dentists, *Community Dental Health*, 6: 44–59.

Rodmell, S. and Watt, A. (1986) *The Politics of Health Education: raising the issues*, London, Routledge and Kegan Paul.

Tones, B. K. (1986) Health Education and the Ideology of Health Promotion: A Review of Alternative Approaches, *Health Education Research* 1: 3–12.

Watt, A. (1986) Community Health Initiatives and their Relationship to General Practice, *Journal of the Royal College of General Practitioners*, 36: 72–73.

9 Pharmacists and Health Promotion

Since the early 1960s community pharmacies have been recognised as being ideally located within the community for the provision of health education (Gatherer, 1966). Both the Nuffield Report and the Government White Paper *Promoting Better Health* have envisaged a development of the role of pharmacists in the community, with pharmacists becoming more involved in advising patients about prescribed and purchased medication and providing advice and education on general health matters. Evidence suggests that this role is complementary to that of general practitioners, with little overlap of roles (Simpson, 1979) and indeed there seems to be a mutual appreciation among pharmacists and general practitioners of their professional functions and their input to health care (Harding and Taylor, 1989a, 1989b).

9.1 PHARMACY-BASED HEALTH EDUCATION CAMPAIGNS

The National Pharmaceutical Association's 'Ask your pharmacist, you'll be taking good advice' campaign, launched in 1983, was the first nationwide attempt to promote pharmacists as providers of health education advice. Television, magazine, leaflet and poster advertisements were employed to encourage people to consult the pharmacist on matters of health education and in particular to seek advice in the treatment of certain symptoms and minor illnesses.

Since 1986 the Department of Health has funded the distribution of health care material by pharmacies through the 'Health care in the high street' (1986) and the 'Pharmacy health care' (1989) schemes. These schemes were joint initiatives of the Royal Pharmaceutical Society of Great Britain, the Health Education Authority, the Scottish Health Education Group, the National Pharmaceutical Association and Family Planning Association and involved the provision of health education literature and display stands to all community pharmacies. Literature supplied through the 'Health

TABLE 9.1 *Nature of enquiries to pharmacists*

Type of enquiry	%
Symptom related	71
OTC medicine enquiry	13
Dispensed medicine enquiry	12
General health enquiry	3
Other	1

Reproduced with permission from Shafford and Sharpe (1989).

care in the high street' scheme has covered a variety of areas including family planning, coronary heart disease, drug abuse, cystitis and AIDS. Surveys have indicated that more than 95 per cent of the leaflets were available in pharmacies (Morley *et al.*, 1987) and that in the two years the 'health care in the high street scheme' ran more than ten million leaflets were distributed (*Pharmaceutical Journal*, 1989a).

Studies of pharmacy health education campaigns have been oriented to the prevention of disease and ill health rather than the promotion of health as such. Health education has thus been rather narrowly defined, focusing on advice on symptoms and enhancing patient compliance. For example, the report, *The Pharmacist as a Health Educator* (Shafford and Sharpe, 1989) concentrated predominantly on advice given by pharmacists relating to symptoms and prescribed and non-prescribed medicines. This extensive survey of 517 community pharmacies in the North East Thames Regional Health Authority has yielded some valuable information on the advisory role of pharmacists. Shafford and Sharpe found that enquiries made of pharmacists by patients and customers fell predominantly into one of four categories, with the great majority of enquiries being related to a particular symptom or set of symptoms (Table 9.1).

In responding to the symptoms presented to them by patients, pharmacists have a role in secondary prevention (see Chapter 8). The most commonly presented symptom was a cough, other prevalent symptoms included eye and skin conditions, diarrhoea and symptoms associated with colds (Table 9.2).

Many general practitioners believe that they are too frequently consulted by the public for treatment for what they consider to be 'trivial conditions' (Cartwright and Anderson, 1981). In responding

✗ TABLE 9.2 *Symptom enquiries presented to pharmacists*

Symptom	% of all symptom enquiries
Cough	14.0
Eye problems	8.0
Skin rash	4.8
Diarrhoea	4.6
Sore throat	4.4
Cold	4.4
Constipation	4.4
Diarrhoea and vomiting	2.8
Ear problems	2.8
Dry, flaky skin	2.6
Others (including headache, muscular pain, fatigue)	48.6

Reproduced with permission from Shafford and Sharpe (1989).

to symptoms, pharmacists may diagnose and if necessary treat a minor ailment by sale of an Over The Counter (OTC) medicine and, where appropriate, refer patients to a general practitioner (Table 9.3). Twenty-six per cent of patients presenting symptoms were advised to see their general practitioner if the symptom persisted. No person presenting a symptom was referred to a self-help group.

In 1988 a Consumers' Association study of advice given by community pharmacists indicated that 'decent advice and professional sympathy are available: in around 40 per cent of cases, pharmacists were rated highly for this; fewer than a fifth were considered poor' (Consumers' Association, 1988). The survey indicated a significant improvement in pharmacists' responses to symptoms compared with similar surveys carried out in 1975 and 1985. The survey suggested, however, that there was still room for improvement and that pharmacists should be aware of the Pharmaceutical Society's

✗ TABLE 9.3 *Pharmacists' responses to symptom enquiries*

Response	% of all symptom enquiries
Sold OTC medicine	76
Gave verbal advice	70
Referred to a general practitioner	17
Gave information leaflet	7

Reproduced with permission from Shafford and Sharpe (1989).

guidelines for responding to potentially serious symptoms. These guidelines, published in 1981 (Pharmaceutical Society, 1981), deal with the general principles involved in responding to the symptoms encountered in community pharmacy. Guidance is given on those symptoms which are most likely to be indicators of serious disease and those which can safely be treated with OTC medication. As we have already seen in chapter three, the majority of symptoms remain untreated or are treated with medicines purchased by or for the sufferer. Pharmacists, then, have an important role in assisting patients with the purchase and use of medicines by supplying appropriate advice and information, whether solicited or not, and by determining if the symptoms experienced by a patient are sufficiently serious to merit a visit to a general practitioner.

Thirteen per cent of enquiries made to pharmacies are related to OTC medicines. A survey of five per cent of all community pharmacies concluded that nationwide more than one million requests were made daily for medicinal products (Phelan and Jepson, 1980). Seventy-four per cent of all OTC medicines are purchased from pharmacies (British Market Research Bureau Ltd., 1987). Over The Counter medicines sold in pharmacies are of two legal categories, as defined by the Medicines Act 1968: 'Pharmacy Medicines' which may only be sold in pharmacies under the supervision of a pharmacist and 'General Sales List' medicines which may be sold in pharmacies or any other retail outlets. Since pharmacies should at all times be 'under the personal control' of a pharmacist, then General Sales List medicines sold in pharmacies are treated differently than when sold from other retail outlets, such as supermarkets or drug stores.

When considering enquiries relating to purchased medication, enquiries relating to cough remedies are most frequently encountered in pharmacies. This corresponds to the symptom most frequently presented to pharmacists (Table 9.4). Eighty-three per cent of all OTC medicine enquiries resulted in the sale of an OTC medicine, whilst verbal advice was provided as a response to 63 per cent of all OTC medicine queries.

Pharmacists are also asked a wide range of questions relating to prescribed and dispensed medicines. This aspect of the pharmacists' activities is frequently ignored, it is a function complementary and additional to that of the general practitioner. Patients may be anxious about their prescribed medication, including the possibility of side-effects, be concerned whether purchased non-prescription

TABLE 9.4 *Over the counter medicine enquiries presented to pharmacists*

OTC medicine	% of all OTC medicine enquiries
Cough remedies	13.8
Analgesics	11.0
Vitamin supplements	11.0
Skin applications	9.2
Travel aids	6.4
Medicines to take abroad	6.4
Laxatives	4.6
Indigestion preparations	3.7
Antihistamines	3.7
Others	30.3

Reproduced with permission from Shafford and Sharpe (1989).

medication will interact with it, or simply uncertain of other aspects relating to the medicine itself or its administration (Table 9.5).

The majority of such enquiries can be dealt with by pharmacists, however on 23 per cent of occasions, in response to such enquiries, patients were referred back to their general practitioners.

In addition to dealing with patient queries, at the point of handing over a dispensed medicine, pharmacists should reiterate the prescriber's instructions and give additional information when

TABLE 9.5 *Dispensed medicine enquiries presented to pharmacists*

Subject of enquiry	% of all dispensed medicine enquiries
Possible adverse reactions	23.4
Availability	10.3
Nature and action	10.3
Effectiveness	10.3
Dosage	8.4
Interactions	8.4
Identification	7.5
Size or colour	6.5
Alcohol allowed concurrently	4.7
Administration	3.7
Others	6.5

Reproduced with permission from Shafford and Sharpe (1989).

considered appropriate. The reinforcement of the prescriber's instructions may enhance the compliance of patients with the prescribed drug regimen. This ability to improve patient compliance is often quoted as an important facet of the pharmacist's role. However it should be appreciated that the reasons for a patient's non-compliance with their prescribed drug regimen are many and varied.

The term 'compliance' is usually employed to describe a patient's use of medication in accordance with the directions of the prescriber. A broader definition might be the extent to which the patient's behaviour appears to be in accord with medical advice; this definition would consider whether patients' lifestyle is also modified in accordance with professional health care advice.

A failure to follow medical advice is termed non-compliance and may be either the result of a conscious decision, for instance deliberately not taking medication, or unintentional due to a lack of appropriate information or a misunderstanding of how to medicate correctly. Failure to comply may have various consequences, including a worsening or lack of improvement in the patient's condition, possibly with a concurrent increase in suffering. Non-compliance may also result in the occurrence of side-effects, drug interactions and overdoses, and will also result in unnecessary wastage of costly health care resources.

It is obviously the responsibility of the prescriber to try to ensure patient compliance. As the pharmacist dispensing medication is the last health care professional patients encounter before commencing their medication, they too may have some influence over patient compliance.

Studies of the general population have indicated that greater than 50 per cent of people fail to comply with prescribers' directions. One such study found that only 22 per cent of patients fully complied with the directions, whilst more than 31 per cent took their medication in a way that was potentially seriously harmful to their health (Boyd *et al.*, 1974).

Rates of non-compliance may be associated with the nature of the therapy. It has been estimated, for example, that 90 per cent of patients using inhaled steroids for the long-term treatment of bronchial asthma fail to comply properly with their prescribed therapy (*Pharmaceutical Journal*, 1989b).

A number of factors have been suggested as contributing to high levels of non-compliance. Some of these are related to the drug and the dosing regimen, including patient misunderstanding of the directions given by the prescriber or on a medicine label, no immediate relief of symptoms, complex drug regimens with a large number of drugs being taken, and the occurrence of side-effects. However, there are also other important factors not directly related to the drug regimen, such as socio-economic factors, patient health beliefs, illness behaviour and the quality of the health professional/patient relationship (Chapter 4). For instance, the belief that a medicine is effective in treating a disease is likely to result in the patient following the prescribed regimen, whilst scepticism or disbelief in the usefulness of medication may result in reduced levels of compliance.

9.2 ENHANCING DRUG COMPLIANCE

Evidence suggests that adequate counselling of patients in the use of their drugs can improve their compliance with the prescribed regimen. One study showed that intensive counselling by pharmacists of previously non-compliant hypertensive patients was effective in bringing about a significant improvement in compliance. On cessation of the counselling programme, however, patients returned to their non-compliant behaviour (McKenney *et al.*, 1973).

The provision of simple comprehensive verbal instructions, devices to remind patients when to take their medicines, and the availability of patient information leaflets may also significantly enhance compliance. The Royal Pharmaceutical Society has advocated the use of such patient information and instruction leaflets to assist patient education and compliance (*Pharmaceutical Journal*, 1986), and the Consumers' Association has also called for printed information on prescribed medication to be made widely available to all patients.

As we have indicated, patient-compliance – like all illness behaviour – is influenced by factors such as social class, ethnic background, financial resources and the patients' level of education and understanding. An appreciation of how these factors influence health and illness behaviour will assist pharmacists in understanding the possible reasons for non-compliance, and may help in educating patients about medicines and the importance of compliance for their health. To achieve this, health professionals will need to communicate effectively to patients, and take into account the patient's circumstances (Dickson *et al.*, 1989). A very small minority of all enquiries made of pharmacists are related to general health matters (Shafford and Sharpe, 1989). Such enquiries are predominantly concerned with weight loss, pregnancy, diet, smoking and family planning. The most frequent response to such enquiries was to give verbal advice, whilst information leaflets were provided as a response to 21 per cent of the consultations. Most consultations between pharmacists and patients relating to general health matters lasted between 5 and 10 minutes. Such a heavy demand on pharmacists' time in addition to normal dispensing activities has serious implications if this aspect of the pharmacist's role in health promotion is to be expanded, as proposed by the Nuffield Report and the White Paper, *Promoting Better Health*. Such an expansion of pharmacists' activities, it has been argued, will necessitate the presence of more than one pharmacist in a pharmacy (Kerr, 1982) or changes in the way pharmacists supervise the dispensing of prescriptions (Pharmaceutical Society, 1988).

9.3   HEALTH PROMOTION STRATEGIES AND DRUG MISUSE

One aspect of health promotion in which pharmacists would seem to have a particularly important role is that of drug misuse. The term 'drug misuse' describes the misuse of purchased or prescribed medicines, and the use of illicit substances. Pharmacists may come into daily contact with people who are misusing a wide range of non-prescription medicines. The products most frequently misused have been identified as Codeine and Phensedyl Linctuses, Kaolin and Morphine Mixture and laxatives (Ball and Wilde, 1989). The Code of Ethics of the Pharmaceutical Profession (Royal Pharmaceutical Society, 1989) indicates that 'A pharmacist should exercise his professional judgement in controlling the purchase of unnecessary and excessive quantities of medicine' and 'a pharmacist should apply additional control over sales of medicinal products known to be likely to cause such difficulties (liable to "abuse"). It is recommended that the products concerned should be sold personally by the pharmacist.' Pharmacists will also be aware of people whom they suspect of dependence on prescribed medication. A number of classes of drugs may cause problems, such as tranquillisers, analgesics and laxatives. In recent years the occurrence of benzodiazepine dependence has caused alarm. As a result the

Council of the Pharmaceutical Society issued a statement (1989) regarding dependence on benzodiazapines as the result of long-term prescribing. Pharmacists are seen as having a mediating role between the patient and prescriber: advising patients to consult their general practitioner for a reassessment of their treatment or, where appropriate, contacting the prescriber personally.

In the past, pharmacists' involvement with intravenous drug misusers was limited, in that they simply supplied prescribed methadone to registered drug misusers in accordance with medically defined 'treatment' programmes involving administration of an opiate substitute.

Since the early 1980s however, there has been a major development in the debate on drugs policy which has involved a shift of emphasis in strategies aimed at drug misusers. Strategies have become more flexible with the realisation that 'treatment' for drug misusers has not proved cost effective, with a considerable number of 'addicts' relapsing after passage through such 'treatment' programmes. The high proportion of 'addicts' who relapsed after 'treatment', added to the pressure of financial cuts in the health service, has contributed to the shift in the debate away from a 'treatment' ethos, and towards a more pragmatic 'harm minimisation' strategy (Advisory Council on the Misuse of Drugs, 1988). Although 'treatment' facilities continue, they frequently operate alongside programmes designed to minimise the harm associated with drug misuse.

This shift in the primary aim of drug policy has complemented the pharmacists' extended role as a community based health care expert. Pharmacists are among a range of health and social service personnel who are increasingly being brought into play to address the issue of drug misuse. If their contribution is to have an impact, it will depend to a significant extent on a comprehensive understanding by the pharmacist of the terminological, historical, social and political issues surrounding the question of drug misuse.

9.4 DRUG MISUSE, AIDS PREVENTION AND PHARMACISTS

Public anxiety over drug misuse has been enhanced, and to an extent overshadowed, by reports that the number of people who had acquired Human Immunodeficiency Virus (HIV) – that is the virus which can lead to their developing Acquired Immune

Deficiency Syndrome (AIDS) – had reached epidemic proportions. Evaluation of an experimental needle exchange scheme
(see below) has indicated that a relationship exists between
needle sharing among drug users and individuals who are HIV
positive, i.e. who have acquired the virus which may lead to
AIDS (Stimson *et al.*, 1988). During the 1980s transmission of
the HIV virus became the most evident type of drug-related
harm. The current wave of public concern over the spread of
AIDS poses a major dilemma for the providers of treatment
for drug misusers. The dilemma involves a conflict between
the traditional goal of drug treatment services – namely working
towards getting individuals drug free – and the ·more pragmatic
goal of 'harm minimisation' – encouraging intravenous drug users
to avoid exposure to the AIDS virus, particularly through sharing
HIV-infected needles and syringes. The debate on drug treatment
provision has developed from the original aim of eradicating drug
misuse, towards 'harm minimisation' by encouraging drug-taking
practices which reduce the risk of contracting AIDS.

One feature of the new strategy for 'harm minimisation' has
focused on health education. High-risk groups, such as homosexuals and intravenous drug misusers in particular, have been
targeted for health education on how the AIDS virus is transmitted
and how the risk of transmission can be significantly reduced. Risk
reduction literature for drug misusers is available from General
Practitioners' surgeries and, since 1988, from community pharmacies. Additionally, the Home Office appointed Advisory Council on
the Misuse of Drugs' report on AIDS has highlighted the potential
role of pharmacists as a source of information on AIDS-related
issues.

9.5   INJECTING EQUIPMENT EXCHANGE SCHEMES

Health education forms one strand of a wider strategy to contain
the spread of AIDS. A more interventionist approach has been
the introduction of 'needle exchange schemes'. In 1987 the Government initiated an experimental scheme to provide intravenous
drug users who were unwilling or unable to stop injecting drugs,
with a supply of sterile needles and syringes. These schemes also
provided drug-related counselling services, HIV testing, and advice
on 'safe sex' practices. Evidence indicates these schemes have led to

a reduction in syringe sharing (Stimson *et al.*, 1988)

Both the Home Office Advisory Council on the Misuse of Drugs, and the Chief Medical Officer of the Department of Health, recognise the unique position community pharmacists hold as a source of information on AIDS-related issues: displaying educational leaflets, promoting the sale of condoms, and providing advice and counselling. A study of community pharmacists in February 1988 (*Pharmaceutical Journal*, 1988) indicated that 62 per cent of pharmacists would be prepared to get involved in selling syringes and needles to drug misusers. A subsequent study found that approximately three quarters of pharmacists questioned were prepared to sell injecting equipment to drug misusers. Around twenty-eight per cent actually sold needles and syringes, whilst three per cent participated in injecting equipment exchange schemes (Glanz *et al.*, 1989). At present, however, pharmacists' involvement is limited to local initiatives working to guidelines provided by the Council of the Royal Pharmaceutical Society of Great Britain (1987). These guidelines, which have been supplemented by a further nineteen-point guideline by Clitherow (1989), advise that pharmacists should exercise their professional judgement in dealing with requests for sterile syringes.

Currently there is no coherent strategy for pharmacists to contribute effectively to preventing the spread of AIDS, nor to contribute to injecting equipment exchange schemes. In purely practical terms, for example, the cost of disposing of potentially contaminated sharps (needles and syringes) from pharmacies is most often met by the pharmacists themselves. Many pharmacists also require further training on the provision of appropriate AIDS advice. Moreover, it is pertinent that drug misusers are unwelcome in some pharmacies, and that the AIDS virus is no longer contained exclusively within minority populations such as intravenous drug-users, haemophiliacs, and homosexuals, but is now increasingly prevalent in the heterosexual population.

Health education and promotion forms a key element of pharmacists' 'extended role'. As we have argued, pharmacists have a clear contribution to make in advising patients and public on the use of purchased and prescribed medication, ensuring patient compliance. There is also potential for the provision of opportunistic community-based health education. Pharmacists' involvement in community-based health education is limited, as yet, and it will only be feasible and effective when a broader concept of health promotion is taken into account. The introduction of 'high street' diagnostic testing has heightened the profile of the community pharmacy as a centre for health maintenance. Pharmacy based 'needle exchange schemes' will also contribute to a public awareness of the health promoting activities of pharmacists.

It is important to recognise that successful health promotion results in an impact on the public's health. The traditional, didactic approach to health education, as we have seen in chapter eight, has limited impact. Health education involves more than simply providing appropriate literature or standard verbal instructions to people. Health and illness behaviour is extraordinarily complex, and is influenced by a person's social environment. With an appreciation of the social processes associated with health and illness behaviour, pharmacists and health planners are more likely, and indeed more able, to develop health education programmes and health promotion that is more appropriate to the needs of the community and thus more effective.

References

Advisory Council on the Misuse of Drugs (1988) *AIDS and Drug Misuse*, London, Department of Health and Social Security.

Ball, K. and Wilde, M. (1989) OTC Medicines Misuse in West Cumbria, *Pharmaceutical Journal*, 242: 40.

Boyd, J. R., Covington, T. R., Stanaszek, W. F. and Coussons, R. T. (1974) Drug Defaulting, Part II: Analysis of Non-Compliance Patterns, *American Journal of Hospital Pharmacy*, 31: 485–91.

British Market Research Bureau Ltd. (1987) *Everyday Health Care, A Consumer Study of Self-Medication in Great Britain*, London, The Proprietary Association of Great Britain.

Cartwright, A. and Anderson, D. (1981) *General Practice Revisited: A Second Study of Patients and their Doctors*, London, Tavistock Publications.

Clitherow, J. (1989) Syringe and Needle Exchange Schemes in Pharmacies, *Pharmaceutical Journal*, 243: 166–168.

Consumers' Association (1988) Over the Counter Advice, *Which?* April, 158.

Council of the Royal Pharmaceutical Society (1987) Guidelines for Pharmacists involved in Schemes to Supply Clean Syringes and Needles to Addicts, *Pharmaceutical Journal*, 238: 481.

Council of the Royal Pharmaceutical Society (1989) Benzodiazepines,

Pharmaceutical Journal, 243: 200.

Dickson, D. A., Hargie, O. D. W. and Morrow, N. C. (1989) *Communication Skills Training for Health Professionals: An Instructor's Handbook*, London, Chapman and Hall.

Gatherer, A. (1966) The Role of Pharmacists in Health Education, *Pharmaceutical Journal*, 196: 313–315.

Glanz, A., Burne, C. and Jackson, P. (1989) Role of Community Pharmacies in Prevention of AIDS among Injecting Drug Misusers: Findings of a Survey in England and Wales, *British Medical Journal*, 299, 1076–1079.

Harding, G. and Taylor, K. M. G. (1989a) The Interface Between Pharmacists and General Practitioners in English Health Centres, *Pharmaceutical Journal*, 243: 549–550.

Harding, G. and Taylor, K. M. G. (1989b) Pharmaceutical Services and Interprofessional Communication in Health Centre Pharmacies *Pharmaceutical Journal*, 242, R21–R22.

Kerr, J. P. (1982) The Role of the Pharmacist in Health Education, *Journal of the Institute of Health Education*, 20, 33–38.

McKenney, J. M., Slining, J. M., Henderson, H. R., Devins, D. and Barr, M. (1973) The Effect of Clinical Pharmacy Services on Patients with Essential Hypertension, *Circulation*, 48: 1104–1111.

Morley, A., Panton, R., Taylor, R. J. and Jepson, M. H. (1987) The Health Care in the High Street Campaign and Participation by Community Pharmacists, *Pharmaceutical Journal*, 239: R19.

Pharmaceutical Journal (1986) Report of the Working Party on Information to Patients, 237: 306.

Pharmaceutical Journal (1988) Survey Shows Most Pharmacists Sell to Addicts, 240: 219.

Pharmaceutical Journal (1989a) Health Care in the High Street, 242: 239.

Pharmaceutical Journal (1989b) Compliance Threat to First Line Asthma Use, 243: 292.

Pharmaceutical Society (1981) Response to Symptoms in General Practice Pharmacy, *Pharmaceutical Journal*, 226: 14–16.

Pharmaceutical Society (1988) Personal Control and Supervision, *Pharmaceutical Journal*, 240: 370–373.

Phelan, M. J and Jepson, M. H. (1980) The Advisory Role of the General Practice Pharmacist, *Pharmaceutical Journal*, 224: 584–588.

Royal Pharmaceutical Society (1989) *Medicines and Ethics, A Guide For Pharmacists*, London, The Royal Pharmaceutical Society.

Shafford, A. and Sharpe, K. (1989) *The Pharmacist as Health Educator*, London, Health Education Authority.

Simpson, R. (1979) Access to Primary Care, *Royal Commission on the National Health Service*, Research paper No.6, London, HMSO.

Stimson, G. V., Alldritt, L. J., Dolan, K., Donoghoe, M. C. and Lart, R. A. (1988) *Injecting Equipment Exchange Schemes. Final Report*, Monitoring Research Group, Goldsmiths' College, University of London.

10 Social Research Methods

When carrying out any type of research a series of choices must be made in response to some preliminary questions which should be asked at the early stage of any such work. These questions include: What is the area of study or investigation? What type of question or problem is the research aiming to address? What research design is most appropriate to this research question? What would be the most appropriate method or methods? What would be the most relevant research tools? How will the data be analysed and interpreted?

It is often stated that the most difficult and yet crucial aspect of research is asking the right question. The form of that question in turn will influence the research methods and techniques later employed. For example, if we were asking 'how many' or 'how often' type of questions – such as how often are pharmacists involved in direct communication with general practitioners? – we might carry out a survey. If we wanted to study in more detail the form of communication and interaction between pharmacists and general practitioners, we might undertake direct observation techniques or use more in-depth and less structured interviews.

For researchers working within the disciplines of the natural sciences, the choice of research strategies is governed by the assumptions of the scientific community. One feature of the natural scientists' activities is that they are dealing with material objects, for example, a chemical structure or a human organ. Moreover, it is assumed that by routine, systematic observation and by careful recording of data, knowledge of the interrelation between material objects is accumulated. As for instance in the discovery and study of the pharmacological actions of a drug on the body, or of the study of the physico-chemical properties of a drug compound. The properties of materials are thus understood and classified, and this classification provides scientists with models with which to understand the actions and properties of similar materials. These models are therefore inextricably linked to the methods that are used to build them. That is to say, the assumptions we hold about materials determine our choice of methodological tools employed to investigate them. The link between our assumptions and our methods of analysis is perhaps a less contentious issue amongst natural scientists than social scientists. This is because social scientists do not necessarily share a common set of assumptions about individuals' social behaviour. Consequently, there is not one single method of social research, but several, each of which assumes a particular theoretical model of social behaviour.

However, irrespective of whether research is in the natural or social sciences, Shipman (1988) suggests that four key questions should be addressed when conducting research.

1. If the investigation were to be carried out again by different researchers, using the same methods, would the same results be obtained?
2. Does the evidence reflect the reality under investigation?
3. What relevance do the results have beyond the situation investigated?
4. Is there sufficient detail about the way the evidence was produced for the credibility of the research to be assessed?

Only by making clear the researcher's assumptions about social behaviour which are implicit in the research methodology will these questions be adequately addressed.

10.1 METHODS OF SOCIAL ANALYSIS

Social research methods can be classified as being either qualitative or quantitative. Although such categories are not mutually exclusive, we shall use this dichotomy to organise the material in this chapter. These divergent approaches adopt different research tools and are based upon, and informed by, different theoretical foundations. The dichotomy, however, is not always clear cut, and quantitative and qualitative methods can often be used in conjunction with one another; they yield different types of data, which may well be complementary.

Quantitative research methods

The purpose of quantitative methods is to generate precise measurements of social action which can be explained by the accumulation of statistical data. Quantitative research aims:

(a) to explain social behaviour in terms of a cause and effect relationship, with the social action as the effect, and an underlying governing principle the cause; for example, it may be argued that juvenile delinquency is caused by poverty.

(b) to measure social behaviour by objective criteria, for example how often a patient consults a pharmacist (a consultation being defined in a set of objective criteria, not as defined by either the patient or the pharmacist).

The experimental method

The experimental method is often used as the organising principle of qualitative research. It implies that the researcher intervenes in a process, the effects of which are then observed and measured. It involves attempts to control all the variables affecting the process being studied, the aim being to identify causal relationships. Researchers begin this type of research by developing theoretical models about the way individuals act under given circumstances, then carry out experiments to test these predictions. To illustrate, it could be hypothesised that the use of fluoride toothpaste will affect the rate of tooth decay in children. Two groups of children would be selected, being matched for age, sex, social class, height, schooling etc., and given a dental inspection. The experimental group is provided with a year's supply of fluoride toothpaste, the control group with ordinary toothpaste. After one year a post-test dental examination finds that the experimental group have significantly less decay. The researchers would then draw conclusions on the basis of this observation.

Qualitative research methods

Many 'real life' situations do not lend themselves to study by precise measurement, and can not be fully understood by the accumulation of statistical data. Qualitative research, by way of direct observation and involvement with people under study, aims for a detailed description and understanding of what people really think, how they structure and organise their thoughts, whence they derive their ideas and how they are likely to act in particular circumstances. The emphasis is on naturally occurring events rather than on the aggregation of observations of a series of behaviours, views or attitudes. The aim of such research is to facilitate an in-depth understanding and an appreciation of the meanings people attach to what they do or believe. Qualitative research aims to elicit:

(a) what people 'really think', whence they derive their ideas and beliefs, how they organise and structure their ideas;

(b) how people act in their 'natural' settings;

(c) social action as it occurs. Unlike in the laboratory it is often unrealistic or impossible to create experimental conditions to control for all, if any, of the extraneous variables; for example it would be virtually impossible to study behaviour at football matches in such a 'controlled' way.

The main research tools of qualitative analyses are:

1. Participant observation – the observer participates in the daily lives of people under study, observing things that happen and listening to what is said and then makes notes of his or her observation. For example, a researcher who spent two years working as an assistant in a youth club found that sharing and eating certain types of sweets was a particularly powerful social practice (James, 1979).
2. Group discussions – the researcher, with the aid of a list of relevant topics, guides the conversation among a small group of respondents. Often the researcher will pursue subjects which emerge spontaneously as well as the pre-defined topics. Warwick *et al.* (1988) used a combination of interviews and group discussions to explore young people's perceptions of AIDS. The responses revealed that a good deal of confusion and uncertainty was felt by these young people, aged 16 to 23.
3. Unstructured or conversational interviews – unlike the questionnaire where the questions are predetermined and are uniform to allow for the aggregation of responses, the interviewer talks with the respondent informally around the topics relevant to his or her research. With the aid of a list of topics, the interviewer pursues subjects as they arise and follows relevant leads. The role of the interviewer is

non-directive and yet not wholly passive, because he or she must assess how what is being said relates to the research focus. Such interviewing requires a great deal of skill and the interviewer needs to be trained. Unstructured interviews have produced a great deal of the data on people's beliefs and conceptualisations of health and illness (see Chapter 4).

Qualitative research is usually small scale and aims at eliciting a richness of detail rather than statistical generalisations – i.e. we can learn a great deal about a particular social situation or how people interact with each other in given situations, but we cannot make claims that the findings would hold true beyond our field of study. Social science has also gained from 'case study' research which often, although not exclusively, uses qualitative research methods. By case study we mean the detailed examination of a single example or case, for instance, a small society, a pharmacy, an organisation, or a health centre. For comparative purposes, a series of case studies may be undertaken.

One of the main advantages of this type of research is that we are able to see people within their natural context. Sociologists, and in particular medical sociologists, in recent years have come increasingly to appreciate the value of being able to relate what people say and do to their individual circumstances.

Ethnography

Ethnography involves more detailed examination of small groups in society. Although sociologists have increasingly adopted this method, it has its roots in anthropological research. The traditional research tool of the ethnographer was participant observation, with the researcher actually living in the society under study. Today the method is used within our own communities and the research involves watching, listening, keeping diaries, examining records, unstructured interviews or conversations. Ethnographic research assumes the importance of people's perspectives, perceptions and actions and the meanings they attribute to these. People's views, beliefs and actions are observed within the context of their every-day lives. The philosophy underlying the ethnographic approach diverges from traditional survey research. The latter is closely allied to the natural sciences in that it is characterised by testing models and hypotheses. Ethnographic research has no clearly defined hypothesis to be tested, rather data are uncovered. Data collection is an exploratory process; it is 'inductive' rather than 'deductive' reasoning which is inherent in such experimental studies. The researcher approaches the subject of the study without predefined ideas or theories. Instead, theories emerge – this is referred to as 'grounded theory' (Glaser and Strauss, 1967), that is, it involves systematically collecting data which is used to develop theories and concepts. This is in contrast to constructing a hypothesis and then testing it with the appropriate data.

10.2 SAMPLING

The most rigorously constructed survey schedule can yield consistently biased data if it is not applied to a representative sample of the population being surveyed. The most elementary sampling technique – selecting a specific number of respondents at random – is no less problematic than more sophisticated procedures such as stratified sampling. This is because sampling, by its nature, always involves an element of bias and error. The principle underlying random sampling is that each unit within the population surveyed has an equal chance of being selected. To illustrate, a random sample of ten pieces of coal selected from a mound would involve more than making a selection from the pieces of coal immediately to hand. The heavier pieces would be more likely to be at the bottom of the pile than the top; pieces in the centre of the pile would be excluded from being selected because they would not be immediately accessible, and so forth. Strictly speaking, then, there is no such thing as a truly 'random sample'. When attempting to draw up a random sample, every attempt must be made to ensure that the elements comprising the population from which the sample is to be taken, whether the sample comprises lumps of coal or patients presenting to a pharmacist, have an equal chance of being selected. For this purpose random tables, which are frequently published in statistical textbooks, may be used as a means of drawing up a random sample.

The decision whether or not to sample, and the choice of sampling techniques will be determined not least by the cost of conducting a survey as well as the demand for accuracy and precision. Only by surveying the total population can the optimum degree of precision be guaranteed. While this may be a viable option for surveys of very small populations, more often the cost of administering the survey to a total population will be prohibitive. A sample will therefore have to be taken. Two popular methods of sampling are:

(a) Simple random sample – involves a random selection of specific number of units drawn from the population investigated which is treated as an undifferentiated whole.

(b) Stratified random sample – involves breaking the investigated population into distinct sub-groups or strata, and then randomly selecting a specific number of units from each strata.

A considerable amount has been written about both the theory and techniques of survey sampling. Selected texts on sampling are outlined at the end of this chapter.

10.3   INTERVIEWS AND SOCIAL SURVEYS

One of the most common forms of data collection in social research is the interview. Much has been written on the nature, types and pitfalls of the interview.

1. *Standardised or structured interview*: this involves eliciting the same information from every respondent. The questions must be designed to ensure that the answers are comparable and classifiable. There are two forms of standardised interviews:

(a) schedule interviews, where the wording and sequence of questions are determined in advance and questions are asked in the same way;

(b) non-schedule interviews, where the questions may be asked in any order, as is considered appropriate by the interviewer during the interview. In this case the interviewer is told the information required and is allowed to vary their order and nature if appropriate.

2. *Non-standardised interview*: these may take many forms, but the interviewer is not restricted to set questions as there is no attempt to gain the same classifiable categories of information from every respondent. Such an interview may take the form of specific open

questions or merely a list of topics to be discussed. There are three important characteristics of this method:

Flexibility – the interviewer must be able to adapt and respond to the individual and their circumstances;

Responsive or interactive – the interviewer must keep alert to pursue interesting ideas or 'leads';

Probing – the interviewer must pursue the respondents' initial reasoning by asking further questions.

This type of interviewing requires a considerable degree of skill and expertise, and it is important that interviewers are suitably trained for this task.

Surveys are a means of collecting information from large samples of the population relatively quickly and efficiently, allowing comparisons to be made between individuals and groups. Conducting a survey requires that the researcher pays particular attention to its design. For instance, it would be necessary to ensure a representative sample is drawn, and that the survey is organised adequately, i.e. that the questionnaire schedule is appropriate, and that researchers are suitably trained.

Social survey interviews involve a structured dialogue: the questions are pre-formulated in order to elicit specific answers. These answers form the social survey data. Success in obtaining the required data depends on asking the appropriate questions. There are two principal considerations to be borne in mind when designing survey questions. First, the question must be clearly intelligible to the respondent. Second, care should be taken to ensure that all respondents could provide an appropriate answer to the question.

Textbooks are available on survey research methods, providing information on how to phrase questions. Whilst the nature of the questions will be governed by the subject of the survey and the population to be surveyed, there are several precepts to be applied when phrasing survey questions. Survey research aims to elicit responses based on a series of specific questions. An ambiguous question may produce an answer based on an idiosyncratic interpretation by the respondent. Such data is unacceptable because the answers would then not be comparable. Technical language has a precise meaning and should be used only if the survey population could be expected to be familiar with it. Otherwise jargon should be avoided as inappropriate. Clarity is important since there is less likelihood that the question will be misinterpreted, however patronising phrasing should be avoided. Questions to which there are a wide range of possible responses, or which combine a number of questions into one, are often difficult to answer, and the responses are even more difficult to analyse. One solution is to provide a checklist of possible responses to a single question together with instruction on the number of responses to be entered. Negatively phrased questions and questions requiring detailed recall by respondents do little to promote accurate answers.

The survey method produces invaluable data for social scientists, but may suffer from being superficial in that it cannot always glean the more subtle aspects of human behaviour.

10.4   SELF-COMPLETED QUESTIONNAIRE SURVEYS

The correct phrasing of survey questions is particularly crucial in the design of a self-completed questionnaire. Questions designed to elicit the attitudes and values of respondents are not likely to produce adequate answers. The reasons for holding particular attitudes and values are often very complex, and cannot be adequately represented from pre-formulated questions. For this reason, many self-completed questionnaires are comprised of a series of 'closed' questions; that is to say questions having a very restricted range of possible responses, for example, 'Have you used this pharmacy before?' To such a question the respondent can only answer 'Yes', 'No' or 'Don't Know'. Similarly, 'Do you prefer tablets or capsules?' is a closed question. Closed questions have the virtue of being easy to answer by the respondent and are relatively simple to analyse.

While the general nature of the questions to be asked will be determined by the subject of the survey, the actual selection of questions should be generated from preliminary studies of the population to be surveyed. Before planning specific questions it is important to establish the possible scope of the issues to be surveyed. This may involve unstructured interviews with a small sample from the proposed survey population. Additional background information may be obtained from a variety of other sources, including previous survey data. The importance of this preliminary work cannot be overstated. Self-completed questionnaire surveys are an unsolicited intrusion on the survey population. It is crucial that the information sought cannot be readily obtained from other sources, and that it will achieve the survey's objective.

Once the questions have been compiled, the completed questionnaire should be 'piloted'. This usually involves administering the questionnaire to a small sample of respondents. The returned questionnaires will highlight any inadequacies in the questionnaire's content and wording, and may indicate any potential difficulties with analysis of the full survey data.

10.5   THE RESPONSE RATE

A postal self-completed questionnaire is effectively unsolicited mail and may be treated as such by the recipient. The success of the survey therefore relies on eliciting the co-operation of the respondent in completing and returning the questionnaire. A number of measures may facilitate an acceptable response rate. These include:

1. Enclosing a stamped addressed envelope
2. Personalising the introductory letter
3. Clearly printing the questionnaire
4. Ensuring the relevance of the questionnaire to the respondent
5. Securing prior approval from any appropriate official body, such as an Ethics Committee
6. Registering the data in accordance with the Data Protection Act
7. Stressing confidentiality of the data and anonymity of the respondent
8. Prior announcement of the study in the appropriate journals.

It is also very important to have a strategy for following up non-respondents to a postal questionnaire survey. At least one reminder should be issued to non-respondents. Further reminders may be issued to persistent non-respondents but are likely to have a markedly reduced effect than the first. An alternative to the second

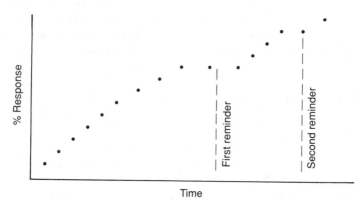

FIGURE 10.1   *Effect of reminders on the response rate*
of self-completed questionnaire surveys

reminder, if at all feasible, is to contact the non-respondent by telephone. A telephone call has the advantage of establishing whether the postal questionnaire was ever received, and whether the respondent actually intends to complete and return the questionnaire. The timing of any strategy for issuing reminders is equally important – if issued too early potential respondents may feel pestered, but if issued too late this may indicate to the respondent the survey's lack of urgency (and possibly its lack of importance) (see Figure 10.1).

10.6   A GUIDE TO SURVEY QUESTION FORM AND CONTENT

Surveys have become a particularly popular method of social research, possibly because of their apparent simplicity. Essentially social surveys simply involve a researcher administering pre-formulated questions to a number of potential respondents. Administering a social survey is indeed relatively straightforward, but the amount and quality of information obtained requires considerable preliminary work if useful and usable data is to be obtained.

There are several mistakes to avoid in the difficult task of constructing survey questions. The suggestions below are not exhaustive, nor are the potential errors indicated necessarily mutually exclusive. It is hoped these will indicate some of the more obvious pitfalls which, with careful planning, can be avoided.

Inappropriate question form

It is important to choose the appropriate form of question closed or open, to elicit the response desired.

    i. 'Do you have opinions on . . . ?' (Closed)
   ii. 'What are your opinions on . . . ?' (Open)

In this example a closed question is an inappropriate form to elicit an opinion. The obvious answer to the closed question is either YES or NO. Either of these answers reveals nothing of the actual opinions held.

Loaded or leading questions

Implicit in these types of question is the desired or expected answer. An example of a loaded question would be, 'Do you consider the National Pharmaceutical Association's "Ask you pharmacist" campaign was a success, or not?'

A leading question may produce more information than a loaded question, though it may not necessarily reflect accurately the individual's true response. For example 'Following the Nuffield Report on Pharmacy do you think the pharmacist should be more involved in advising patients on their medicines?'

Two questions in one

'Does having a pharmacy within the health centre make querying a prescription with the prescriber easier, and has this benefited the patient?'

'Do you think aspirin and paracetamol are appropriate treatments for migraine?'

Double negative

'Do you consider not contacting the prescriber about a potential drug interaction on a prescription is unprofessional?'

And taking things to extremes: 'Do you not consider not continuing to take a prescribed antibiotic is an inappropriate response to failure of the medication?'

The answer, 'Yes' or 'No', to such questions may not convey what the respondent actually believed.

Complex questions

'If doctors are going to be held responsible for their own budgets, do you believe that pharmacists with their knowledge of drug costs, should have a more interactive role with prescribers at the point when a prescription is written, or not?'

Abbreviations, jargon or technical language

'Do you keep PMR's in this pharmacy?'

'How great has the trend towards OPD affected the role of the community pharmacist?'

Abbreviations such as 'PMR' and 'OPD' may be confusing to the respondents and consequently the benefits of using a shortened question are outweighed by the risks of eliciting a confused or inappropriate response.

'After inhaling your bronchodilator aerosol, do you hold you breath for five seconds before exhaling?'

Terms such as 'inhaling' and 'exhaling' may not be clearly understood by respondents not acquainted with medical terminology. The question loses nothing by replacing these words with 'breathing in' and 'breathing out'. The word 'bronchodilator' could be omitted altogether. Similar confusion may arise over the use of such terms as 'fracture', 'gastro-intestinal', 'regimen', etc.

Conversational

'How do you find you get on with the general practitioners?'

'Do you employ a general assistant to help out in the dispensary?'

In these examples 'get on' and 'help out' are not defined. The answers to these questions are not comparable because there is no shared definition between respondents.

Ambiguous questions:

'How long has the pharmacy been open?'

Though the question is clearly designed to establish the duration in months and years, the question may invite the facetious answer: 'Since 8.30 this morning, as usual!' Another example of ambiguity is contained in the question 'How long have you worked in this pharmacy?':

0 – 5 years
5 – 10 years

10 – 20 years
20 years or more?

The question clearly poses a problem for respondents for whom the answer is 5, 10 or 20 years.

Vagueness and Imprecision
'How long have you been a pharmacist?'
This will elicit useful information, but by careful forethought more detailed or precise information could be obtained, by for instance asking 'When did you first register as a pharmacist?'
'How long have you worked full-time, i.e. 30 hours or more per week, in this pharmacy?'
The following question is similarly flawed: 'How frequently do you (the pharmacist) and the prescriber consult with each other?'
The response to this question will simply be the sum total of all consultations between pharmacist and prescriber. It will yield no information as to who initiated the consultation.

Hypothetical Questions
It is important from the outset that it is realised that such questions can only elicit attitudes and opinions, not factual information.
'Do you think pharmacists should have access to patient medication records held by the prescriber?'

Meaningless or inappropriate questions
'Is the *Pharmaceutical Journal* as good as the *Chemist and Druggist*?'
The aims and content of the two journals are completely different and therefore one is not an appropriate alternative to the other.

10.7 ANALYSING DATA

Computer programmes designed to analyse survey data have developed rapidly in recent years. In the past, computer processing and analysis of data often involved the use of mainframe computer programmes only. Today, however, such programmes have been developed to run on personal computers thus making the task of data processing and analysis quicker and easier. Indeed, one such programme, the Statistical Package for the Social Science (SPSS) has been designed specifically to handle social survey data.

Computer handling of survey data requires each of the responses to the survey to be coded in such a way that they can be read by the computer programme. The techniques for coding survey questions is covered comprehensively in the literature outlined in the further reading section at the end of this chapter, and recent software developments have made the process of entering coded data relatively straightforward. Moreover, these programmes can perform a myriad of statistical analyses on the data, but ultimately it is up to the researcher to make sense of the findings. The sheer complexity and power of these programmes can be seductive, and a range of statistical tests may be applied to the data simply because they are available. Often such a plethora of results may be a hindrance rather than a help in making sense of the data. For this reason, it is useful to consider when planning the survey what statistical tests are necessary to meet the survey's objectives.

People using a computer to store details of any living person are now required to register with the Data Protection Registrar, in accordance with the Data Protection Act (1984). Although the majority of institutions holding computer records of their personnel are already registered, if the institution wishes to obtained data for research purposes, details of the information to be collected, together with those who will obtain it, are required to be registered with the Data Protection Registrar.

10.8   VALIDITY AND CAUSALITY

The reliability and validity of accumulated data are fundamental to good research.

Reliability concerns the extent to which measurements if repeated under the same conditions yield the same results; for example, if a standardised interview was administered by different interviewers the same results should be produced.

Validity refers to the extent to which the research instruments, or measures, measure what they purport to measure. Quite clearly the extent to which one's research results are valid is of paramount importance.

It is important to note that reliability and validity are not necessarily synonymous; for example, an intelligence test may be reliable in that it produces consistent results, but it may not be measuring intelligence as was understood in the research hypothesis; and as such the results may be invalid. There are many different types of validity (Cook and Campbell, 1979). It is important to distinguish between internal and external validity. Internal validity concerns whether the research method employed is actually measuring the phenomenon being investigated. External validity concerns the extent to which the research results can be generalised beyond the population studied. For instance, a survey of people's attitudes to pharmacies conducted within pharmacies may be 'self-selecting', in that only the attitudes of those people who visit a pharmacy will be measured, and the attitudes of those who do not will be excluded. One strategy to enhance the level of external validity in survey research involves sampling procedures. The main sampling strategies have been discussed above.

Experimental and survey research involves a process of ruling out plausible alternative explanations, such that, '. . . the only process available for establishing a scientific theory is one of eliminating plausible rival hypothesis' (Cook and Campbell, 1979). This is what the philosopher, Karl Popper termed 'falsification' or the 'hypothetico-deductive method'. The 'hypothetico-deductive' method involves first establishing a hypothesis, drawn from interviews, observations and such like, which could be refuted empirically, i.e. it is 'testable'. If a hypothesis continues to hold, despite experiments designed to disprove it, it becomes accepted as a 'deductive causal' explanation, though not as proof. To illustrate this point Popper uses the example of a swan. We may wish to hypothesise that all swans are white. To test this hypothesis empirically, we may conduct an exhaustive search of many swans, and find without exception that all swans we have observed are indeed white. Our findings therefore allow the hypothesis to stand. However we have not proved all swans are white, only that we have been unable to refute the hypothesis. The discovery of a single black swan would be sufficient to reject the hypothesis.

The implications for research which relies exclusively on statistics are considerable. For example, statistical correlations, based on the types of surveys we have described, in many ways provide the starting point for the development of theories and explanations. Social research involves trying to 'explain' these findings, e.g. ill-health is significantly (statistically) associated with poverty. However, it is crucial not to get carried away by statistical relationships, for it is all too easy to fall into the trap of making 'invalid' assumptions about the relationship between two variables. Researchers usually seek to understand the casual connections between variables which change simultaneously.

To illustrate this, variable A (excessive consumption of animal fats) may be associated with variable B (heart disease). In a study, we want to elicit which variable is 'responsible' or 'independent' and which is 'dependent'. We need to be certain which is the independent and which is the dependent variable, i.e. does A cause B or B cause A? If we were to say that A (excessive consumption of animal fats) was the independent variable and B heart disease was the dependent variable, that is A causes B, we would need to meet at least three basic criteria to ensue that this statement was valid.

1. Correlation: an association between two variables must be statistically significant. For instance, self esteem may be found to vary with educational achievement.
2. Time: we must be sure that the independent variable is prior to the dependent variable. For example, did the school child feel a failure because she failed her exams or did she fail her exams because she felt a failure? Such problems could easily confound a study of educational achievement, especially if the study was retrospective.
3. Extraneous factors may affect both A and B. Thus we cannot assume a simple causal relationship between A and B. For instance, poor educational achievement (B) may be assumed to be dependent on a child's low self esteem (A). However, both poor educational achievement and low self-esteem may be influenced by a third variable such as poor housing (X).

Perhaps our main point is that to create a 'causal model' is an extremely precarious process in social research and it is always to a greater or lesser extent circumscribed because (a) it is impossible to set up an experiment with water-tight control groups; and (b) in sociology we are dealing with human beings whose actions, unlike the actions of chemicals, are influenced by how they make sense of their surroundings and their interpretations of happenings around them.

Another problem in establishing causal models to understand the social world is the multiplicity of factors involved in social processes, for example the social factors which affect people's health.

10.9 SOME USEFUL ADDRESSES

Considerable amounts of information of relevance to the social aspects of pharmacy practice research can be gathered from a range of data collecting bodies.

The Government Statistical Service (GSS)
The Government Statistical Service is the largest single supplier of statistics in the United Kingdom. Although it exists to service the needs of the government, the GSS publishes a range of social statistics, including data on health and personal social services. Details of GSS publications are available from the Central Statistical Office, Great George Street, London SW1P 3AQ.

The Office of Population Censuses and Surveys (OPCS)
The Office of Population Censuses and Surveys; St Catherine's House, 10 Kingsway, London WC2B 6JP is one of the largest data collection agencies and contains all published census data from the United Kingdom, dating back to 1801. Statistics relating specifically to population and health from 1837 onwards are also available.

The Data Protection Registrar
The Data Protection Registrar can be contacted at: PO Box 66, Wilmslow, Cheshire SK9 5AX. Tel. 0625 535777.

The Health Education Authority
The Health Education Authority, Hamilton House, Mabledon Place, London WC1H 9TX has a comprehensive library of publications relating to health issues. It also publishes the *Health Education Journal*.

The Consumers' Association
The Consumers' Association, 2 Marylebone Road, London NW1 4TX, publishes *Which?* magazine and has published reports on health care services for consumers.

Further Reading

General Source texts

A list of social science based projects undertaken in health care research is to be found in: *The Medical Research Directory*, (1983) Chichester, John Wiley and Sons. The British Sociological Association, Medical Sociology Group, have published *Medical Sociology in Britain; A Register of Research and Teaching* (5th edition, 1986) (eds) D. Field and S. Platt. This contains information on current research in the sociology of health care, and the researchers names and addresses. The Central Statistical Office, Great George Street, London SW1P 3AQ annually publishes a general digest, *Social Trends* containing health related-data on, for example, patient consultation rates with health professionals, annual number of prescriptions dispensed, and data on health service resources such as manpower, and average cost per prescription.

Methodological aspects of social surveys

Hoinville, G. and Jowell, R. (1983) *Survey Research Practice*, London, Heinemann Educational Books.

Marsh, C. (1982) *The Survey Method: the contribution of surveys to sociological explanation*, London, George Allen and Unwin.

Moser, C. A. and Kalton, G. (1983) *Survey Methods in Social Investigation*, Gower, Aldershot.

Ethnographic research

Hammersley, M. and Atkinson, P. (1983) *Ethnography: Principles in Practice*, London, Tavistock Publications.

Research design

Hakin, C. (1987) *Research Design*, London, Allen and Unwin.

References

Cook, T. D. and Campbell, D. T. (1979) *Quasi-Experimentation: Design and Analysis Issues for Field Studies*, Chicago, Rand McNally.

Glaser, B. G. and Strauss, A. L. (1967) *The Discovery of Grounded Theory: Strategies for Qualitative Research*, Chicago, Aldine.

James, A. (1979) The Culture of Kets, *Journal of the Anthropological Society*, 10: 83.

Shipman, M. (1988) *The Limitations of Social Research*, London, Longman.

Warwick, I., Aggleton, P., and Homans, H. (1988) Constructing Common Sense – Young People's Beliefs About AIDS, *Sociology of Health and Illness*, 10: 213–233.

Bibliography

Advisory Council on the Misuse of Drugs (1988) *AIDS and Drug Misuse*, London, Department of Health and Social Security.

Ackernecht, E. W. (1947) The Role of Medical History in Medical Examination, *Bulletin of the History of Medicine*, 21.

Allen, G. (1985) *Family Life: Domestic Roles and Social Organisation*, Oxford, Basil Blackwell.

Apple, D. (1960) How Laymen Define Illness, *Human Behaviour*, 1: 219–225.

Ball, K. and Wilde, M. (1989) OTC Medicines Misuse in West Cumbria, *Pharmaceutical Journal*, 242: 40.

Becker, M. H. (1974) *The Health Belief Model and Personal Health Behaviour*, New Jersey, Charles B. Slack Inc.

Behavioural Sciences Group (1987) *Compendium of Behavioural Science Teaching at Medical and Dental Schools in the United Kingdom*, University of Glasgow.

Berger, P. (1966) *Invitation to Sociology: A Humanistic Perspective*, Harmondsworth, Penguin.

Bewley, B. R., Higgs, R. H. and Jones, A. (1984) Adolescent Patients in an Inner London General Practice: Their Attitudes to Illness and Health Care, *Journal of the Royal College of General Practitioners*, 34: 543-546.

Black, J. and Laws, S. (1986) *Living with Sickle Cell Disease*, London, Sickle Cell Society.

Blane, D. (1985) An Assessment of the Black Report's Explanation of Health Inequalities, *Sociology of Health and Illness*, 7: 423-445.

Blaxter, M. (1983) The Causes of Disease: Women Talking, *Social Science and Medicine*, 17: 59-69.

Bloor, M. and Horobin, G. (1975) Conflict and Conflict Resolution in Doctor-Patient Interactions, in Cox C. and Mead M. E. (eds.) *A Sociology of Medical Practice*, London, Collier-Macmillan.

Blumhagen, D. (1980) Hyper-Tension: a Folk Illness with a Medical Name, *Culture, Medicine and Psychiatry*, 4: 197-227.

Boyd, J. R., Covington, T. R., Stanaszek, W. F. and Coussons, R. T. (1974) Drug Defaulting, Part II: Analysis of Non-Compliance Patterns, *American Journal of Hospital Pharmacy*, 31: 485-91.

British Market Research Bureau Ltd (1987) *Everyday Health Care, a Consumer Study of Self-Medication in Great Britain*, London, The Proprietary Association of Great Britain.

Calnan, M. (1984) The Health Belief Model and Participation Programmes for the Early Detection of Breast Cancer: A Comparative

Analysis, *Social Science and Medicine*, 19: 823-830.

Cartwright, A. (1967) *Patients and their Doctors: A Study of General Practice*, London, Routledge and Kegan Paul.

Cartwright, A. and Anderson, D. (1981) *General Practice Revisited: A Second Study of Patients and their Doctors*, London, Tavistock Publications.

Catford, J. and Nutbeam, D. (1984) Towards a Definition of Health Education and Health Promotion, *Health Education Journal*, 43: 38.

Chrisman, N. J. (1977) The Health Seeking Process: An Approach to the Natural History of Illness, *Culture, Medicine and Society*, 1: 351-377.

Clitherow, J. (1989) Syringe and Needle Exchange Schemes in Pharmacies, *Pharmaceutical Journal*, 243: 166-168.

Consumers' Association (1988) Over the Counter Advice, *Which?* April, 158.

Cook, T. D. and Campbell, D. T. (1979) *Quasi-Experimentation: Design and Analysis Issues for Field Studies*, Chicago, Rand McNally.

Council of the Royal Pharmaceutical Society (1987) Guidelines for Pharmacists involved in Schemes to Supply Clean Syringes and Needles to Addicts, *Pharmaceutical Journal*, 238: 481.

Council of the Royal Pharmaceutical Society (1989) Benzodiazepines, *Pharmaceutical Journal*, 243: 200.

Dale, J. R. and Appelbe, G. E. (1989) *Pharmacy Law and Ethics*, London, Pharmaceutical Press.

Department of Health (1989) *Working for Patients*, (Cmd 555), London, HMSO.

DHSS (1976) *Prevention and Health: Everybody's Business: A Reassessment of Public and Personal Health*, London, HMSO.

DHSS (1976) *Priorities for Health and Personal Social Services in England*, London, HMSO.

DHSS (1976/77) *First Report from the Expenditure Committee, session 1976/77 Preventative Medicine Volume 1 Report*, London, HMSO.

DHSS (1986) *Primary Health Care: An Agenda for Discussion* (Cmd 9771), London, HMSO.

DHSS (1988) *Promoting Better Health*, (Cmd 249), London, HMSO.

Dickson, D. A., Hargie, O. D. W. and Morrow, N. C. (1989) *Communication Skills Training for Health Professionals: An Instructor's Handbook*, London, Chapman and Hall.

Donovan, J. (1984) Ethnicity and Health: a Research Review, *Social Science and Medicine*, 19: 663-670.

Dubos, R. (1959) *Mirage of Health*, New York, Harper and Row.

Ehrenreich, J. (ed.) (1978) *The Cultural Crisis of Modern Medicine*, London, Monthly Review Press.

Elworthy, P. H. (1986) The Pattern of Women Pharmacists, 1966 to 1983, *Pharmaceutical Journal*, 237: 218-224.

Fagin, L. (1984) *The Forsaken Families: the Effects of Unemployment on Family Life*, Harmondsworth, Penguin.

Farrant, W. and Russell, J. (1985) *Health Education Council Publications: A Case Study in the Production, Distribution and Use of Health Information*. Final Report of the Health Education Publications Project, Institute of Education, University of London.

Fitzpatrick, R., Hinton, J., Newman, S., Scambler, G. and Thompson, J. (1984) *The Experience of Illness*, London, Tavistock.

Freidson, E. (1961) *Patients' Views of Medical Practice*, New York, Russell Sage Foundation.

Freidson, E. (1970) *Professional Dominance*, Chicago, Atherton Press.

Freidson, E. (1970) *Profession of Medicine; A Study in the Sociology of Applied Knowledge*, New York, Dodd, Mead and Co.

Freidson, E. (1975) Dilemmas in the Doctor-Patient Relationship, in Cox, C. and Mead, A. (eds.) *A Sociology of Medical Practice*, London, Collier-Macmillan.

Gatherer, A. (1966) The Role of Pharmacists in Health Education, *Pharmaceutical Journal*, 196: 313-315.

Gershuny, J. (1983) *Social Innovation and the Division of Labour*, Oxford, Oxford University Press.

Glanz A., Burne, C. and Jackson, P. (1989) Role of Community Phramacies in Prevention of AIDS among Injecting Drug Misusers: Findings of a Survey in England and Wales, *British Medical Journal*, 299, 1076–1079.

Glaser, B. G. and Strauss, A. L. (1967) *The Discovery of Grounded Theory: Strategies for Qualitative Research*, Chicago, Aldine.

Goldberg, E. M. and Morrison, S. L. (1963) Schizophrenia and Social Class, *British Journal of Psychiatry*, 109: 785-802.

Goode, W. J. (1960) Encroachment, Charlatanism and the Emerging Profession: psychiatry, sociology and medicine, *American Sociological Review*, 25: 902-914.

Gordon, G. (1966) *Role Theory and Illness: a Sociological Perspective*, New Haven, College and University Press.

Graham, H. (1984) *Women, Health and the Family*, Brighton, Wheatsheaf Books.

Hannay, R. (1979) *The Symptom Iceberg: a Study in Community Health*, London, Routledge and Kegan Paul.

Harding, G. (1988) Patterns of Heroin Use: What Do We Know? *British Journal of Addiction*, 83: 1247-1254.

Harding, G. (1988) Behavioural Science and Pharmacy, *Pharmaceutical Journal*, 242: 124.

Harding, G. and Taylor, K. M. G. (1988) Pharmacies in Health Centres, *Journal of the Royal College of General Practitioners*, 38: 566-567.

Harding, G. and Taylor, K. M. G. (1989) The Interface Between Pharmacists and General Practitioners in English Health Centres, *Pharmaceutical Journal*, 243: 549-550.

Harding, G. and Taylor, K. M. G. (1989) Pharmaceutical Services and Interprofessional Communication in Health Centre Pharmacies *Pharmaceutical Journal*, 242, R21-R22.

Hargie O., Sanders C. and Dickson, D. A. (1987) *Interpersonal Communication Skills*, London, Croom Helm.

Holland, W. W. and Walker, J. (1971) Population Studies in the London Borough of Lambeth, *Community Medicine*, 126, 153.

Illich, I. (1974) *Medical Nemesis*, London, Calder Boyars.

Illich, I. (1975) *Limits to Medicine*, London, Marion Boyars.

Illsley, R. (1986) Occupational Class Selection and the Production of Inequalities in Health, *Quarterly Journal of Social Affairs*, 2: 151-165.

James, A. (1979) The Culture of Kets, *Journal of the Anthropological Society*, 10: 83.

Jamous, H. and Peloille, B. (1970) Changes in the French University Hospital System, in Jackson, J. A. (ed.) *Professions and Professionalisation*, Cambridge, Cambridge University Press.

Joelson, L. and Wahlquist, L. (1987) The Psychological Meaning of Job Insecurity and Job Loss: Results of a Longitudinal Study, *Social Science and Medicine*, 25: 179-182.

Johnson, T. (1989) *Professions and Power*, London, Macmillan Education Ltd.

Jones, D. R. (1978) Errors on Doctors' Prescriptions, *Journal of the Royal College of General Practitioners*, 28: 543-545.

Kassebaum, G. G. and Baumann, B. O. (1965) Dimensions of the Sick Role in Chronic Illness, *Journal of Health and Human Behaviour*, 6: 16–27.

Kerr, J. P. (1982) The Role of the Pharmacist in Health Education, *Journal of the Institute of Health Education*, 20, 33-38.

King, M. D. (1968) Science and the Professional Dilemma, in Gould J. (ed.), *Penguin Social Sciences Survey, 1968*, Harmondsworth, Penguin.

Klein, R. (1983) *The Politics of the National Health Service*, London, Longman.

Klein, R. (1989) *Politics of the National Health Service*, London, Longman. (second edition)

Koos, E. (1954) *The Health of Regionsville: What the People Felt and Did About It*, New York, Columbia University Press.

Lapsley, R. (1988) Prescription Monitoring in a Nursing Home, *Pharmaceutical Journal*, 240: 688.

Le Grand, J. (1982) *The Strategy of Equality*, London, Allen Unwin.

Littlewood, R. and Cross, S. (1980) Ethnic Minorities and Psychiatric services, *Sociology of Health and Illness*, 2: 2.

MacIntyre, S. (1988) A Review of the Social Patterning and Significance of Measures of Height, Weight, Blood Pressure, and Respiratory Function, *Social Science and Medicine*, 27: 327-337.

Maclure A, Stewart, G. T. (1984) Admissions of Children to Hospital in Glasgow: Relation to Unemployment and Other Depravation Variables, *Lancet* ii: 682-688.

Marbach, J. J. and Lipton, J. A. (1978) Aspects of Illness behaviour in Patients with Facial Pain, *Journal of the American Dental Association*, 96: 630-638.

Marmot, G. G., Adelstein, A. M. and Bulusu, L. (1984) Immigrant Mortality in England and Wales, *Population Trends*, London, HMSO.

Marmott, M. and Theorell, T. (1988) Social Class and Cardiovascular Disease: The Contribution of Work, *International Journal of Health Services*, 18: 659-674.

McEwan, J. (1983), Pharmacy in Inner City Areas: Opportunities for Health Education, *Pharmaceutical Journal*, 231: 346-348.

McKenney, J. M., Slining, J. M., Henderson, H. R., Devins, D. and Barr, M. (1973) The Effect of Clinical Pharmacy Services on Patients with Essential Hypertension, *Circulation*, 48: 1104-1111.

McKeown, T. (1979) *The Role of Medicine: Dream, Mirage or Nemesis*, Oxford, Blackwell.

McKinlay, J. B. (1973) Social Networks, Lay Consultations, and Help-Seeking Behaviour, *Social Forces*, 51: 255-292.

Mechanic, D. (1968) *Medical Sociology: A Selective View*, New York, Free Press.

Mechanic, D. and Volkart, E. (1960) Illness Behaviour and Medical Diagnosis, *Journal of Health and Human Behaviour*, 1: 86-94.

Meredith Davies, J. B. (1983) *Community Health, Preventative Medicine and Social Services*, London, Bailliere Tindall.

Morgan M., Calnan, M. and Manning, N. (1985) *Sociological Approaches to Health and Medicine*, London, Routledge and Kegan Paul.

Morgan, M. and Watkins, C. J. (1988) Managing Hypertension Beliefs and Responses to Medication among cultural groups, *Sociology of Health and Illness*, 10: 561-578.

Morley, A., Panton, R., Taylor, R. J. and Jepson, M. H. (1987) The Health Care in the High Street Campaign and Participation by Community Pharmacists, *Pharmaceutical Journal*, 239: R19.

Morrow N. C., Speedy, P. and Totten, C. (1986) Health Education Perspectives in Continuing Education Programmes for Pharmacists, *Health Education Journal*, 45: 166-170.

Nettleton, S. J. (1986) Understanding Dental Health Beliefs: an Introduction to Ethnography, *British Dental Journal*, 161: 145-147.

Nettleton, S. J. (1989) Dentists and Dental Health Education: a Study of the Perceptions of 28 Community Dentists, *Community Dental Health*, 6: 44-59.

Neville, R. G., Robertson, F., Livingston, S. and Crombie, I. K. (1989) A Classification of Prescription Errors, *Journal of the Royal College of General Practitioners*, 39: 110-112.

Nuffield Committee of Inquiry into Pharmacy (1986) *Pharmacy: a Report to the Nuffield Foundation*, London, Nuffield Foundation.

OPCS (1982) Mortality Statistics 1978, London, HMSO.

OPCS (1986) Registrar General's Decennial Supplement on Occupational mortality 1979-1983, London, HMSO.

Parsons, T. (1939) The Professions and the Social Structure, *Social Forces*, 17: 457-467.

Parsons, T. (1951) *The Social System*, London, Free Press.

Patrick, D. and Scambler, G. (eds.) (1986) *Sociology as Applied to Medicine*, London, Bailliere Tindall.

Pharmaceutical Journal (1986) Report of the Working Party on Information to Patients, 237: 306.

Pharmaceutical Journal (1987) Survey of Pharmacists, 238: 685.

Pharmaceutical Journal (1988) '3000 Average.', 240: 175.

Pharmaceutical Journal (1988) Residential Home Staff Need Help from Pharmacist, Study Finds, 240: 217.

Pharmaceutical Journal (1988) Six Million Chances Daily for Health Education, 241: 179.

Pharmaceutical Journal (1988) Survey Shows Most Pharmacists Sell to Addicts, 240: 219.

Pharmaceutical Journal (1989) Pharmacist Liable for Doctor's Error, 243: 186.

Pharmaceutical Journal (1989) Compliance Threat to First Line Asthma Use, 243: 292.

Pharmaceutical Journal (1989) Health Care in the High Street, 242: 239.

Pharmaceutical Society (1981) Response to Symptoms in General Practice Pharmacy, *Pharmaceutical Journal*, 226: 14-16.

Pharmaceutical Society (1988) Personal Control and Supervision, *Pharmaceutical Journal*, 240: 370-373.

Phelan, M. J and Jepson, M. H. (1980) The Advisory Role of the General Practice Pharmacist, *Pharmaceutical Journal*, 224: 584-588.

Rathwell, T. and Phillips, D. (eds.) (1986) *Health, Race and Ethnicity*, London, Croom Helm.

Roberts, D. (1988) Dispensing by the Community Pharmacist: an Unstoppable Decline? *Journal of the Royal College of General Practitioners*, 38: 563-564.

Rodmell, S. and Watt, A. (1986) *The Politics of Health Education: raising the issues*, London, Routledge and Kegan Paul.

Rosenstock, I. (1966) Why People Use Health Services, *Milbank Memorial Fund Quarterly*, 44: 94-127.

Royal Pharmaceutical Society (1989) Narrow but Clear Majority for No Confidence Motion, *Pharmaceutical Journal*, 242: 438.

Royal Pharmaceutical Society (1989) *Medicines and Ethics, A Guide For Pharmacists*, London, The Royal Pharmaceutical Society.

Scambler, A., Scambler, G. and Craig, D. (1981) Kinship and Friendship Networks and Women's Demands for Primary Care, *Journal of the Royal College of General Practitioners*, 26: 746-750.

Shafford, A. and Sharpe, K. (1989) *The Pharmacist as Health Educator*, London, Health Education Authority.

Shipman, M. (1988) *The Limitations of Social Research*, London, Longman.

Shuval, J. T. (1981) The Contribution of Psychology and Social Phenomena to an Understanding of the Aetiology of Disease and Illness, *Social Science and Medicine*, 15: 337-342.

Simpson, R. (1979) Access to Primary Care, *Royal Commission on the National Health Service*, Research paper No.6, London, HMSO.

Social Trends (1988) London, HMSO.

Stacey, M. (1988) *The Sociology of Health and Healing*, London, Unwin Hyman.

Stimson, G. V. and Webb, B. (1975) *Going to See the Doctor*, London, Routledge and Kegan Paul.

Stimson, G. V., Alldritt, L. J., Dolan, K., Donoghoe, M. C. and Lart, R. A. (1988) *Injecting Equipment Exchange Schemes. Final Report*, Monitoring Research Group, Goldsmiths' College, University of London.

Stone, P. and Curtis, S. J. (1989) *Pharmacy Practice*, London, Farrand Press.

Szasz, T. S. and Hollender, M. H. (1956) A Contribution to the Philosophy of Medicine: the Basic Models of the Doctor-Patient Relationship, *Archives of International Medicine*, 97: 585-592.

Taylor, J. (1979) Hidden Labour in the National Health Service, in: Atkinson, P, Dingwall, R, and Murcott, A. (eds.) *Prospects for National Health*, London, Croom Helm.

The National Health Service (General Medical and Pharmaceutical Services) Amendment Regulations 1985.

Thompson, E. P. (1977) *The Making of the English Working Class*, Harmondsworth, Penguin.

Thunhurst, C. (1985) *Poverty and Health in the City of Sheffield*, Environmental Health Dept. Sheffield City Council.

Tones, B. K. (1986) Health Education and the Ideology of Health Promotion: A Review of Alternative Approaches, *Health Education Research* 1: 3-12.

Townsend, P. and Davidson, N. (1982) *Inequalities in Health: the Black Report*, Harmondsworth, Penguin.

Townsend, P., Phillimore, P., and Beattie, A. (1986) *Inequalities in Health in the Northern Region: an Interim Report*, Northern Regional Health Authority and the University of Bristol.

Turner, B.S. (1987) *Medical Power and Social Knowledge*, London, Sage Publications Ltd.

Wadsworth, M., Butterfield, W. and Blaney, R. (1971) *Health and Sickness: The Choice of Treatment*, London, Tavistock Publications.

Wadsworth, M. E. J. (1986) Serious Illness in Childhood and its

Association with Later Life Achievements, in Wilkinson R. G. (ed.) *Class and Health: Research and Longitudinal Data*, London, Tavistock.

Waldron, I. (1983) Sex Differences in Illness Incidence, Prognosis and Mortality: Issues and Evidence, *Social Science and Medicine*, 17: 1107-1123.

Warwick, I., Aggleton, P., and Homans, H. (1988) Constructing Common Sense – Young People's Beliefs About AIDS, *Sociology of Healt'ı and Illness*, 10: 213-233.

Watt, A. (1986) Community Health Initiatives and their Relationship to General Practice, *Journal of the Royal College of General Practitioners*, 36: 72-73.

Whitehead, M. (1987) *The Health Divide: Inequalities in the 1980s*, London, Health Education Council.

Williams, G. H. and Wood, P. H. (1986) Common Sense Beliefs about Illness: a Mediating Role for the Doctor, *Lancet* ii, 8522: 1435.

Working Party on Social and Behavioural Science (1989) London, The Royal Pharmaceutical Society.

Wright, P. (1979) A Study of the Legitimisation of Knowledge: the Success of Medicine, the Failure of Astrology, in Wallis R. (ed.) *On the Margins of Science*, Sociological Review Monograph 27, Keele.

Wright-Mills, C. (1959) *The Sociological Imagination*, New York, Oxford University Press.

Zborowski, M. (1952) Cultural components in response to pain, *Journal of Social Issues*, 8: 16-30.

Zola, I. K. (1966) Culture and Symptoms, an analysis of patients presenting complaints, *American Sociological Review*, 31: 615–630.

Zola, I. K. (1973) Pathways to the Doctor: from Person to Patient, *Social Science and Medicine*, 7: 677-689.

Index

135